D0107248

OMG!
Guys

How to Survive 101 of the Most F'ed Dating Situations

Jodi Miller

adamsmedia
Avon, Massachusetts

Published by Adams Media,
a division of F+W Media, Inc.
57 Littlefield Street, Avon, MA 02322. U.S.A.
www.adamsmedia.com

ISBN 10: 1-4405-1266-3
ISBN 13: 978-1-4405-1266-7
eISBN 10: 1-4405-2498-X
eISBN 13: 978-1-4405-2498-1

Printed in the United States of America.

10 9 8 7 6 5 4 3 2 1

Library of Congress Cataloging-in-Publication Data
is available from the publisher.

This publication is designed to provide accurate and authoritative information with regard to
the subject matter covered. It is sold with the understanding that the publisher is not engaged
in rendering legal, accounting, or other professional advice. If legal advice or other expert
assistance is required, the services of a competent professional person should be sought.
—From a *Declaration of Principles* jointly adopted by a Committee of the
American Bar Association and a Committee of Publishers and Associations

Many of the designations used by manufacturers and sellers to distinguish their product are
claimed as trademarks. Where those designations appear in this book and Adams Media was
aware of a trademark claim, the designations have been printed with initial capital letters.

Certain sections of this book deal with activities that would be in violation of various fed-
eral, state, and local laws if actually carried out. We do not advocate the breaking of any
law. The authors, Adams Media, and F+W Media, Inc. do not accept liability for any injury,
loss, legal consequence, or incidental or consequential damage incurred by reliance on the
information or advice provided in this book. The information in this book is for entertainment purposes only.

This book is available at quantity discounts for bulk purchases.
For information, please call 1-800-289-0963.

This is dedicated to my girls, JRC, SGS, and MFM, who helped me through all the *OMG! Guys* moments in my life. Well, maybe not all of them since they're all married and I'm still single and living with a cat.

~JM

contents

chapter 1

Guy Meets Girl

1. You're the only one out of your friends who doesn't have a boyfriend

It's a great time in your life. You're single, carefree, and independent. Life is good. You and your girls are livin' it up. But lately you've noticed that the number of girls that go out on "girls' night" is getting smaller every week. Your weekends, which once resembled an episode of *The Hills*, now more closely resemble *The Golden Girls*. One by one your single girlfriends are becoming one half of a couple. The next thing you know you look around and you're the last single girl in your crew. OMG!

→ **OPTION #1**

Find a guy fast. Monkey see, monkey do right? Follow your friends' lead and get a man. Shit, get a few men if you want. That way, when your friend suggests a couples' night you'll be more concerned with what to wear than how you'll ever get a date.

→ **OPTION #2**

Find new friends. If all your friends are taken, go out and find some new single girls to roll with. Shouldn't be too hard—go through your FB friends and see how many of those people you barely talk to anymore list their status as "single." And hey, most likely your "coupled friends" will become single again soon enough. If not, at least you'll have new single girls to take to the wedding and take advantage of the open bar with.

→ OPTION #3

Stay strong. So what if you're the only one without a boyfriend? Don't get a lame boyfriend just to fit in with your friends. If you like being single right now, then stay single. Just because someone is in a relationship doesn't necessarily mean they're happy. I bet most of your friends will envy the fact that you don't have a guy to answer to. Live it up, sister.

In the Future...

Keep an ex in the mix for last-minute dates. Nothing wrong with recycling your men. Go Green!

2. You don't have the guts to talk to guys

You're out for happy hour with a few of your girls and you see *him* across the room. So cute. You keep looking over at him to see if he notices you. The next time you look over, your eyes lock. He smiles at you. You smile back. He finishes a beer, then starts walking your way and you . . . run to the bathroom and vomit. OMG, this happens every time. Every time you meet a boy you might want to get to know your palms start to sweat, your heart races, and then bam, you either run away or puke. How attractive.

→ OPTION #1

Grow a pair. Seriously, what's the worst that can happen? He's not gonna grab your boob in the middle of a bar (unless you ask him to). So unless you've lost the ability to talk to another person, open your mouth and try to eke out something that sounds half-intelligent.

→ OPTION #2

Get wasted. Okay maybe not wasted, but have a drink before you make contact just to take the edge off. Careful, though. Too many rum and Cokes and you'll throw up on yourself or him. It's hard to get past that.

→ OPTION #3

Practice makes perfect. Start flirting with guys you're not interested
in—you'll feel less pressure and
get your sea legs. Once you've
gotten the swing of things, move
on and up from there. And who
knows? Maybe you'll end up
with one of your practice dudes.
Win, win.

→ OPTION #4

Become a nun. The only time
you'll have to worry about talking to your man is when you're
praying.

OMG Facts for the Shy Girl

Use these quick tips to overcome
an uncomfortable situation.

- **Smile** to show you're friendly.
- **Make eye contact** to show
  you're confident.
- **Sit up straight** to show off
  your boobs.

OMGJesus!

3. You think every guy you meet is a loser

He has no sense of humor. He thinks everything's a joke. His teeth are too big. His hands are too small. His hair is too long. Every time you meet a guy there's always something that you can't stand. He lives too far away. He lives with his parents. Whatever the reason, it seems you just can't meet someone you like. Too picky? Maybe. Getting lonely? Definitely.

→ OPTION #1

Lower your standards. Seriously, if you are finding the smallest things to pick on then maybe the problem is you. Make a list of what you're really looking for in a guy and make sure shit like "his teeth aren't the right size" isn't on it.

→ OPTION #2

Try him out. So maybe at first you don't feel it, but maybe after a date or two you will. Remember what your mother always said: How do you know if you don't like

something if you haven't tried it? So go ahead, take a bite.

→ OPTION #3

Mix it up. Start hanging out with different friends and at different places. If you love hiking and bicycle riding you're probably not gonna meet your dream man passed out at a bar. Join a club that really interests you and hopefully you'll meet someone with similar tastes. If you're interested in finding a drunk, then stick with the bar.

→ OPTION #4

Call in the pros. If you're old enough to use a cell phone while driving, you're probably too old to meet your dream guy at a mall. So if you can't seem to meet a guy you like on your own, go to the professionals. Like online dating, speed dating, or even a real matchmaker (*The Millionaire Matchmaker* if you can afford it, though that bitch seems kinda crazy). True, you're paying money for someone else to find you a guy—but it's their problem now!

> I like the bad-boy types. Generally the guy I'm attracted to is the guy in the club with all the tattoos and nail polish.
> Megan Fox

OMG Dating Tip: Not So Great Places to Meet Guys

- AA meetings
- Unemployment office
- A local middle school (unless you're *both* students)
- The dollar store (if the guy isn't going to shell out for brand name toilet paper, he's probably not going to buy you dinner anyplace without a drive-through)
- Prison (unless you're one of those chicks who marry guys on death row, still, I don't encourage it)

OMG Rant!

Why do people always say that a wedding is a great place to meet a guy? This is bullshit. First of all, almost everyone at the wedding is with a date. And if they are alone, there's usually a reason. Either they're not old enough to date or they're one of the groomsmen which means their only intention that night is to get wasted and try to hook up with anything that has a vagina. I have been to 57 weddings, a bridesmaid 10 times, maid of honor 3 times, and the number of times I have met an available man adds up to zero. The numbers don't lie. So unless you're looking for a statutory charge or a one night stand, forget this myth about bagging your dream guy at your cousin's wedding.

>>>> 4. The guy you've been flirting with all night drops the girlfriend bomb

He's cute and funny and you two have been talking since the moment you met. He comments on what a great smile you have. You both giggle at each other's stupid jokes. You casually touch his arm. He flirtatiously touches your back when he excuses himself "to go take a piss" (okay, he's still a guy). Totally psyched, you text your friend who is watching you from across the room. "OMG, this guy is awesome."

Then all of a sudden, in the middle of his hilarious story about falling asleep on the subway and waking up at the last stop, he drops the bomb. "So there I am, completely lost in the middle of the sketchiest neighborhood, and I have to call my girlfriend to pick me up at two in the morning." Hold on, what? Did you hear him correctly? He *must* have said "my ex-girlfriend." So you ask him, "Oh, did you say your girlfriend picked you up?" "Yeah," he replies. "She's so great. You two would definitely get along."

WTH? How is this happening? He was so obviously sending the signs that he was into you. What an asshole. And what a waste of a night.

→ OPTION #1

Smile and leave. Quickly end the conversation and excuse yourself. He's either oblivious to the signs of flirting or he is planning on cheating on his girlfriend. Either way, this is not the guy for you. Find the next available guy and then make out your cares away.

→ OPTION #2

Confront him. Ask him straight out why he has been so flirty with you all night if he has a girlfriend. He'll probably play the dumb guy act. But whether or not he's aware of it, this asshole has been coming across as not only single but also available. Order a drink on his tab and rejoin your friends. Then stare daggers at him the rest of the night. You know, like the mature adult that you are.

→ OPTION #3

Teach him a lesson. Go from "fun flirt" to DTF right before his eyes. Make suggestive comments about your underwear. Ask him how far away his place is. Press up against him next time you laugh at one of his jokes. Then, right before he thinks you're about to leave together, rip him a new asshole about the dangers of leading girls on *and* cheating on your girlfriend. Leave him and his blue balls on his own.

That'll teach him.

5. You've been talking to a guy for hours and he doesn't ask you for your number

Boy meets girl. Boy and girl start a dialogue. Girl giggles at boy's dumb jokes. Boy listens to girl talk about her cat. Boy asks girl for her number. Except he hasn't. You and this very cute dude have been chatting up a storm all night and you're ready for him to ask, "Can I call you sometime?" but he doesn't. And now he's leaving.

→ OPTION #1

Ask him for his digits. Even though you've been talking all night, boys are dumb. This one, for whatever reason, might be scared of being rejected. Take the initiative and tell him you have to run but you would love to talk again or maybe grab coffee sometime. Give him your number and then peace out. The ball is in his court and now he knows how you feel. If he doesn't feel the same way, you and your girlfriends can overanalyze why he doesn't call over several nights and several (dozen) bottles of wine.

→ OPTION #2

Get clever. Ask if you can see his iPhone cause you're thinking about switching plans. When he forks it over, put your number in there. When you hand it back to him, say something witty like, "Wow, your phone comes with my number already in it. What a great app." A little ballsy, sure, but shit, he's obviously a wuss so you better get used to it.

→ OPTION #3

Cut and run. If he hasn't asked you for your digits, this likely means one of two things: He likes you but isn't ready to date or he is already taken. Either way, you don't need to waste your time. Say goodbye and leave.

If he really wants to call you, he'll stop you and ask for your number.

→ OPTION #4

Start sobbing uncontrollably. When he asks what's wrong, tell him you're dying from a horrible disease and your last wish was to have a guy ask for your number just one more time. He'll feel so bad for you, he'll gladly ask you. The only way this can go wrong is if you end up dating and he wonders why you're still alive after a couple years.

6. You can't decide if the guy you just met is so awesome or if you're just so drunk

He seems funny and cute. You guys are really hitting it off and the sparks are flying. Plus you're actually attracted to him. Then you slam down another shot and you're even *more* attracted to him. Wait . . . are you really into this guy or has Jack Daniels affected your judgment? This all seems very familiar. You meet a guy after you've had a couple of drinks, you think he's amazing until you see him again sober, and then you realize he's a loser. OMG, how can you tell if you really like this one?

→ OPTION #1

Ask your friends. They don't want you to hook up with a troll either so go find out from them what they think of this guy. Unless they're drunk, too, then that probably won't work. In fact, it could backfire and they might like him *too* much. They may end up stealing him, those drunk hoes!

→ OPTION #2

Stop drinking and start sobering up—now. Drink a lot of water and try to clear your head. Invite him to go get something to eat. If you are still into him after the fog clears, there's your answer. If not, run out and leave him with the bill. He'll probably still be drunk so he won't care.

→ OPTION #3

Do nothing. Carpe diem! If you like this dude now, have fun. If in the morning light you notice that he's totally creepy and has an enormous hairy mole on his face, say goodbye for good. Then go out and find another. If this keeps happening, eventually you will find one you still like come morning. Question is, will they still like you?

In the Future...

Try just smoking pot. Makes everyone interesting all the time.

OMG disclaimer: OMG does not endorse doing any drugs. But if you got a prescription card, share the wealth!

Wine	Good conversation, maybe exchanging numbers
Brandy	Holding hands and slow dancing
Beer	Dancing and making out by the bathroom
Whiskey	Dancing, making out *on* the bar, and maybe some groping
Frozen drink	Crying about your last boyfriend and throwing up
Jägermeister	Screwing in the bathroom
Tequila	Blacking out and not knowing anything except that you've done something horrible

7. You and your friend both like the same guy

You and your BFF are out having a great girls' night, when you see him. Tall, dark, and yummy. He smiles in your general direction and makes his way over. After a little while of flirting with you both, he goes to the bathroom and at the same time, you and your friend call, "Shotgun!" You both start laughing . . . until you realize you're both serious. "I think we have a real connection," you say. She comes back with, "Really? Cause I think *we* have a real connection." Game on.

→ OPTION #1

Back down. Look, maybe your friend hasn't had sex since Bush was in office. If that's the case, let her have him. Be the bigger girl here and go find another guy. Unless he clearly decides he wants you—then screw her. All is fair in love and war!

→ OPTION #2

Fight it out (not literally, unless you want to look like you're on an episode of *Teen Mom*). Just decide that you will *both* keep on doing what you're doing and see who comes out victorious. However, promise each other that you'll be happy for the other if they win this battle. If he doesn't ask either of you for your number, assume he's gay and just thought you were both fabulous.

→ OPTION #3

Fight it out. Literally. Make it a cage match and charge money. Whoever is left standing, wins. Let's get ready to R-U-M-B-L-E!

→ OPTION #4

Hoes before bros. If you can't decide who saw him first, then you should both retreat. No reason to let a guy come between you two. Go find two available boys and get busy!

→ OPTION #5

Threesome anyone? If you're both game, then go for it. Trust me, he won't complain. But will you ever be able to look your friend in the eye after you've seen her O face?

In the Future...

Only hang out with ugly chicks.

>>> 8. Your mother won't stop fixing you up

Your mother has always wanted only the best for her little girl. She thinks she knows what's best for you, and most of the time she does. But lately she's been playing the part of matchmaker. In fact, every time she meets someone who has a son around your age she can't help but set you up with him. You've gone out with Louis the lawyer who still lives at home. Trent, the pharmacist's son, who has a bad case of psoriasis. Kim Lee, the dry cleaner's son, who never says more than two words at a time. And, oh yeah, Noah the son of the butcher who might be a serial killer. What to do when your mom is determined to find you a man?

→ OPTION #1

Cut the cord. Sit her down and explain that while you appreciate her help, you can find a guy on your own. When she shakes her head in disbelief, assure her that if you need her help, you will ask. She might start crying but Mommy Dearest needs to learn when to butt the F out.

→ OPTION #2

Move. If you live in another city it will be much harder for her to fix you up. Sure, it'll also be hard living in a strange city where you know no one, but desperate times call for desperate measures.

→ OPTION #3

Hire a guy. Tell her you started dating someone you really like so she should stop fixing you up. Then bring your boyfriend-for-hire to dinner one night. Make sure he mentions that he travels a lot so she doesn't constantly wonder where he is. Then when you do meet a real guy you like, fake the breakup and start dating the new guy.

→ OPTION #4

Beat her at her own game. Maybe she's so concerned with your love life 'cause she doesn't have one of her own. Start setting her up with every guy over fifty-five you can find. Unless she's still married to your father—then it might not go over too well.

You look healthy.	You look fat.
What happened to that nice guy, what's his name? You know, the tall one, the doctor—Steven was it? He was a lovely man.	Stop being so damn picky. You want to end up an old maid?
You are not getting any younger, you know.	At this rate, you stand a very good chance of dying alone with no husband and no kids in a pool of your own vomit.
That is a very *interesting* outfit.	You're dressed like a whore.

>>> 9. You always say the weirdest things when you meet a guy you like

It's always the same thing. You meet a guy and start talking. He seems interested in you and things are going well. Then before you can stop yourself you're telling him about getting your period at the gym during spin class, which is at least better than the time you got the shits during yoga. I mean there you were downward dog and . . . OMG STOP! It's like diarrhea of the mouth, pun intended. There is such a thing as an edit button and yours is apparently broken.

→ OPTION #1

Laugh it off. The next time you catch yourself saying something strange, stop it and start laughing. Cover your ass by saying something like "Just kidding, imagine if I was serious? You ready for another drink?"

→ OPTION #2

Stick to your guns. Look, if this is who you are, then this is who you are. If you're the kind of person who lets every thought fly out of your mouth, better he know now. Maybe one day you'll meet the guy who finds that refreshing, or maybe just a guy who's deaf.

→ OPTION #3

Stop talking. Guys love the silent type; they think it's mysterious. Just nod and smile.

Appropriate Small Talk

- Traveling
- Hobbies
- Apples and oranges. Are they really *that* different?
- That great little farmer's market down the street from your place that you just *love!*
- Chaos theory

Inappropriate Small Talk

- Your latest colonoscopy
- Your latest Pap smear
- Religion
- That funny story about the time you shit your pants

>>> 10. You have profiles on no less than thirty dating websites and *still* can't find a guy

Match.com, EHarmony, Jdate, Desperategirl.com, you're on them all. If a new one pops up, you join. You figure you'll cover all your bases and get a boyfriend in no time. But the same thing keeps happening; you fill out your profile, post your cutest photos, and wait. Nothing. No matches, no e-mails, no winks. OMG, even in cyberspace you're destined to be single!

→ OPTION #1

Expand your search. Expand your dating radius to a larger distance. Yeah, it's hard to date someone who lives a few towns away but that's why we have cars and public transportation. Get a second date before you start worrying about who's going to move to whose town.

→ OPTION #2

Stop wasting your time on the computer and try going out and meeting a real live guy. In this day and age we're too busy texting, tweeting, and searching the Internet for friends and lovers that we forgot what it is like to go out and have actual contact with another person. Get out there; it's a brave new world!

→ OPTION #3

Give your profile a makeover. If your profile reads the same boring shit as every other girl on there it will be hard to stand out. Take some new fun photos and spice up your profile. Say things like, "I hate filling out profiles but I love margaritas and salsa dancing."

That sounds fun, yes?

>>> 11. A guy you just met at the bar tries to have sex with you in the parking lot

Isn't it great when you go out and meet a cute guy? He's fun and interesting and seems really into you. You exchange numbers and he politely asks if he can walk you to your car. As you make your way through the parking lot, you start to anticipate the kiss goodbye. He leans in and you start kissing, but then the kissing starts to get a little hotter and heavier. He suggests you move things to inside your car. Okay, a little groping is nice too. But—oh no. It soon becomes clear he wants to have sex in the parking lot. OMG!

→ OPTION #1

Slam on the brakes. Be strong and say no. If you even seem a little hesitant in your resistance, he'll use this as an in, literally. If he still tries to convince you, ram your knee into his balls. Trust me, he won't want to have sex after that.

→ OPTION #2

Keep driving. Look, you have a decision to make here. A f#*k in the road, if you will. If you like this guy and you're okay with the possibility of never seeing him again, then climb aboard and enjoy the ride.

→ OPTION #3

Flip the switch. Tell him you were hoping this would happen, that you came out tonight just to meet a guy to screw in the parking lot with. This is your favorite parking lot for banging strangers' brains out. Then add, "I'm pretty sure I'm not in the middle of a breakout right now. The cream really seems to be working!" He should be out of the car before you can take off your bra.

→ OPTION #4

Start crying. That will freak him out and maybe he'll want to console you. Men love broken women.

Best Places to Do It

- Bed
- Closet
- Kitchen table
- On a mountain top

Worst Places to Do It

- In prison
- Anywhere that's broadcast on the Internet
- In a Smart Car

12. Your online dating website is telling you to settle

You filled out your profile, uploaded your picture, and you're ready to go. Your online dating website promises to send what they consider to be your matches each week to help you meet that someone special. But apparently the dating website thinks you've aimed a little too high, 'cause the matches they're sending you are not really matches at all. All the guys are out of your age range, out of your driving radius, and hardly meet any of the qualifications you listed on your "want" page. Okay, so maybe you're a little picky but the last match they sent you was a sixty-five-year-old man who lives 100 miles away, but hey, he's a nonsmoker so MATCH!

→ **OPTION #1**

Contact the website. Look, you're paying for this service. You should get what you want. They're basically telling you that your standards are too high and maybe you're reaching for someone out of your league, and that's bullshit. They should never tell you that; that's what your mother is for!

→ OPTION #2

Cancel it. Cancel your membership and try some live one-on-one interaction, like speed dating. At least with that you get the disappointment over with in two minutes.

→ OPTION #3

Take the hint. Maybe this website knows something you don't. Maybe this retired man they want you to meet is filthy rich and is just looking for someone like you to spend his money on.

Hey, it could happen.

Are You Too Picky?

You might be, if you find yourself thinking:

- Nine inches? Not bad, but I'll hold out for a 10.
- Tall, dark, and handsome isn't good enough. Tall, dark, and handsome *with* a trust fund? That I can get into, maybe.
- Sorry, handsome and mysterious sax player. I only date guys who play the oboe.

OMGjesus!

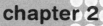

chapter 2

Mr. Right—
or Mr. Right Now?

OMG!

13. Your friends keep fixing you up with losers

"Trust me he's a great guy!" How many times have you heard that? Your friends always want to play match-maker with you, but the problem is that they always fix you up with the biggest losers. One guy popped a zit in front of you; one guy asked if you were into *Star Wars* sex battles; and one guy confessed he was gay, on the date! OMG! People say you can tell a lot about what your friends think of you by the guys they fix you up with and apparently they think you're a loser.

→ OPTION #1

Get new friends. Apparently your friends either only know losers or they have no idea what your taste is. Either way they obviously don't really care about you. So dump them and get new friends. Hot friends, 'cause everyone knows good looking people hang together.

→ OPTION #2

Stop going. Just cause they've fixed you up with these trolls doesn't mean you have to go. Say thank you, but no thank you. You would rather polish off a bottle of cheap wine and watch a *Real Housewives of New Jersey* marathon. Sounds good to me.

→ OPTION #3

Change. Maybe it's not your friends, maybe it's you. If your friends keep fixing you up with losers then take the hint. Try some new hobbies, get a haircut, and lose the "poor me" attitude. *Then* see who your friends set you up with.

→ OPTION #4

Change them. So what if he's a loser? Find the one thing he has going for him and work up from there. Maybe find a loser with money, then buy him some new clothes (and some for yourself, of course). A new look can do wonders for both the guy and you. Careful, though, if you make him over too well, another girl might steal him away.

>> 14. You can never get to the second date

It's always the same thing. He asks you out; you go and have what you consider to be a great first date. Great conversation. Great kiss goodnight, the promise of a phone call soon, then nothing. No call, no text, no second date. Did your deodorant wear off? Was your breath offensive? Did you appear too needy? If it only happened once or twice you could blow it off, but lately it happens every time. You just can't seem to make it to date number two and now you're pissed and more than a little concerned!

→ OPTION #1

Ask them WTF is up. Call one of the dates and straight up ask him. Look, it's not going anywhere anyway so you have nothing to lose. Just be nice and honest and ask him to be honest with you. But be careful what you ask for, the answer he gives you could send you into a drinking binge.

→ OPTION #2

Ask a friend. The next date you have, bring a friend. Have them sit close by and listen in. Maybe you're sending off a strange vibe or maybe you're sending off a strange body odor. Whatever it is, maybe your friend can help. Don't invite them into the makeout session of the date, 'cause that's a threesome. Unless you're into that.

→ OPTION #3

Do nothing. Maybe it's really not you and maybe it's the guys. We tend to attract the same type of guy so try mixing it up a little. If you normally go out with the pretty boy who says all the right things, why not go out with the out of shape, funny guy. ←

At least you'll be laughing.

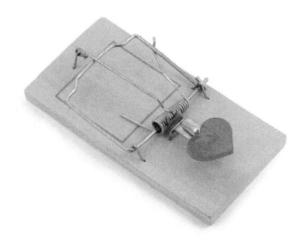

>> 15. Your dog hates him, and she likes everyone else

From the moment they laid eyes on each other, you knew there would be trouble. The death stares, the heavy breathing, the growling. Your sweet little doggie hates your boyfriend and you just can't understand it. Your dog loves everyone, even the homeless dude in front of your supermarket who yells at you. Everyone, that is, except your boyfriend. In fact, every time he even puts his hand on you the dog starts barking. OMG, what's wrong with this bitch?

→ OPTION #1

Heel. Time to get tough, on your dog that is. Keep enforcing the upper hand here. You're the master and this is a dog. Take control and show this bitch who's boss.

→ OPTION #2

Get Cesar! If Option #1 doesn't work, you'll have to call in the professional. You probably won't be able to get Cesar "Dog Whisperer" Millan, so just go down to your local Petco or go online and find a dog trainer. That should give you the skills to help your dog and your guy become BFFs.

→ OPTION #3

Get rid of the dog. If they really can't get along and you love your boyfriend, you might have to say goodbye to your furry friend. After all, only one of those two is going to have sex with you. Give your pooch to a relative or close friend so you can still visit and get ready to get it on with your new man.

In the Future...

Get a cat.
They hate everyone.

→ OPTION #4

Get rid of the guy. Look, dogs have great radar when there's trouble. This might be your dog's way of telling you to get the hell out of this relationship. If she's never let you down before, you might want to follow the dog's advice and kick your dude to the curb.

16. You get set up with someone you've already hooked up with

Your friend tells you all about this smart, good looking, tall, and funny guy from her office she would love to set you up with. He sounds perfect. Normally, you would ask to see a picture of him but your friends have raved about him so much you figure he must be easy on the eyes. So you agree to meet him, and set up a date. Wearing your most flattering dress, you walk into the restaurant where what could be your new Prince Charming awaits. As you get closer, you realize something. This is no new Prince Charming at all. In fact, you've already been out with this dude—and after what you thought was a great date, you slept with him. And Prince Charming never called you again!

→ OPTION #1

Don't mention it. It's been a few years since you guys had that one date so he might not even remember. He was pretty wasted. Then, unless you could really use a free meal, excuse yourself to go the ladies' room and get the hell out of Dodge.

→ OPTION #2

Slap him. He was a total jerk and he deserves a good slap for saying that you had "big calves." You'll never forget that horrible line. Asshole.

→ OPTION #3

Second time is a charm. Give the guy another chance. Tell him where you know him from and see if he apologizes. People change, and maybe you two will get along nicely this time. After all, you have changed quite a bit yourself over the last few years. Just think about how you wore your hair back then. What were you thinking?

→ OPTION #4

F with his head. If he doesn't remember, remind him that you went out before and tell him that you are glad that you ran into him because the night you guys went out, you got pregnant— with his baby. Congrats, Daddy!

17. The date has been over for hours but he won't leave

He parked the car and walked you to your door. He asked if he could come in for a little bit, so you say okay. He's nice and the date was fine but now it's over and apparently he didn't get the memo. You try all the subtle moves, like, "Boy am I tired" and, "I have a big day tomorrow, I should get some sleep" but he's still not leaving. OMG, how the hell do you get him out of there?

→ **OPTION #1**

Be direct. He's a total moron and doesn't get all of your "subtle" hints or he just doesn't care. Either way it's time to put your foot down. Tell him, "thanks for a nice night but it's time for you to go now." If he still tries to stall and stay a little longer, then it's time to put your foot down again, on his ass, on the way out.

→ **OPTION #2**

Go to sleep. Just excuse yourself, go in your room, and go to bed. He'll get the hint when you don't come back. Make sure you lock your bedroom door unless you want him to come in and cuddle.

→ OPTION #3

Freak him out. Start acting like a very obsessive girlfriend and say things like, "this date was amazing, I can't wait to introduce you to my parents," or, "I'm so happy you like my place so much, I was thinking we should move into together." If he's like most guys, he'll be running out the door like his ass is on fire.

→ OPTION #4

Light his ass on fire. For real. Okay, maybe not the best idea but it will definitely get him to leave.

→ OPTION #5

Have sex with him. Trust me, he'll be gone right after he's done.

OMG in Real Life

I once had a guy over for some take-out and wine. Nice guy, but it was getting late and I really wanted him to go. I tried every subtle thing I could do. I took off my makeup, got into my flannel pajamas, brushed my teeth, but this dumbass still didn't get it. I was desperate. I went out to the hallway while he was in the bathroom and pulled the fire alarm. Drastic I know, but it worked. Everyone had to evacuate, and once we all realized it was a false alarm I raced back upstairs. That was our last date.

—Marci

18. Your date has six drinks . . . *before* dinner

He shows up at your house with his own six-pack of beer. He knocks back two martinis while you're waiting to get a table, then polishes off more than his half of the bottle of wine you "share" during dinner. Now, he's getting a little louder and a little more touchy. Before you know it, he's groping the waitress, starting fights with other people, and asking if he can see your tits. Yep, it's official: your date is wasted and guess what? He drove.

→ **OPTION #1**

Take his keys. He will probably fight you for them but you need to make sure he doesn't try to drive. Take his keys and hide them or if you're able to, drive yourself. Take his keys and car and drop his drunken ass off. Then park his car somewhere it will either get towed or where he won't be able to find it.

→ **OPTION #2**

Take him home. If you think you might like this guy, take him with you. Let him pass out on your couch, then make him feel horrible about this the next morning. Guilt can be a wonderful thing, and I bet you'll get breakfast out of the deal.

→ OPTION #3

Pass him off. Just hand his drunken ass over to the bouncer at the bar—they deal with this shit all the time. If he's really that drunk, he might start a fight and get his ass kicked. That's a lesson he won't soon forget. And hey, maybe you'll get a pity f#@k from the hot bouncer. Score!

OMG in Real Life

It was a blind date and from the beginning it wasn't going well. He must have been very nervous because he drank a lot. Before dinner, during dinner, after dinner, and I think he even took a swig in the bathroom. Anyway, I couldn't let him drive so I brought him back to my place, where he proceeds to piss in my plant. When I screamed, "Hey asshole, stop pissing in my plant," he turned to me and said, "Bitch." I was enraged! I told him to get out to which he replied, "Fine, I'll leave but that means we're not having sex tonight." I was shocked by that response, but then I suddenly broke out into laughter and decided to let him pass out on my couch. In the morning, he woke up feeling horrible—and not just from his ungodly hangover. He apologized and quickly left, but later that day I received a dozen roses and a new plant to replace the one he pissed in. We just celebrated our tenth wedding anniversary.

—Dana

In the Future...

Maybe suggest a place that doesn't serve alcohol for the first date. If you make it to the second date, then get drunk together.

19. His credit card gets declined and you're stuck with the $150 dinner tab

Finally. A real guy who takes you out to a nice romantic dinner. A good bottle of wine and great food—you even split dessert. How perfect. You're just thinking to yourself, This guy is amazing. Maybe I'll forgo that "no sex on the first date" rule this one time. . . . Then the waiter comes back with the bill and your date's Visa. Looking pissed, he spits out, "Your card was declined." OMG. You think to yourself, please make an excuse about how it must be the bank's mistake and pull out another card and be done with it. But no card comes out. That's his only card, his credit *and* debit card. He has no money and no way to pay. Guess who's paying for dinner?

→ **OPTION #1**

Break out the cash. If you're smart, you will pack an emergency card in your purse, for unplanned cab rides and so on. And this is one of those emergencies. Pay for dinner and then demand oral sex. Tit for tat.

→ **OPTION #2**

Think fast. Scream at the top of your lungs and yell RAT. Then jump up onto your chair. Start a restaurant-wide panic. While all the waiters are scurrying around grab your date and run. Dishonest? Yes. Exciting? Absolutely.

→ OPTION #3

Bail. Excuse yourself to go to the bathroom while he figures out his next move and take off. Look, you don't want to start a relationship with someone who obviously has money problems.

Unless he's an artist. Everyone knows artists make being poor look sexy.

→ OPTION #4

Do nothing. He's the one who wined and dined you, damn it. Let him figure out how to get out of this mess. Just sit back and continue drinking. Shit, order another drink.

→ OPTION #5

Work it out. What is the restaurant gonna do, make you wash dishes? Have your guy give them his info and promise he will come back with some cash. Then consider the date over.

>>> 20. He expects you to go Dutch

He picked you up. He opened the car door. He chooses the restaurant and suggested a nice bottle of wine. What a gentleman. The date is going quite nicely when then comes that time. The waiter drops the bill. You smile and say thank you for dinner, to which he replies, "You're welcome. Your half comes to $48.12." He smiles, takes out some cash, and looks at you to do the same. Is he serious? Funny, you don't remember showing anyone your passport but apparently you're going Dutch!

→ OPTION #1

Laugh it off. Start laughing, almost inappropriately loud. Say something like, "Oh, you are so funny. You almost had me there," and excuse yourself to the ladies room. As you are getting up, say, "Thank you again for dinner. Very sweet of you." Then hide out in the can 'til the bill is paid.

→ OPTION #2

Pay up. This sucks but at least you know now who you're dealing with. And you also now know how the date is ending.

→ OPTION #3

Make a scene. Start yelling at him at the table. Scream things like, "You want me to split the bill? This is our first date and you except me to pay?!" Then remind him that he picked this overpriced piece of shit restaurant and if you knew you were going Dutch you would have picked McDonalds. Then start crying. He will be so embarrassed that he probably will pay the whole bill. You most likely will never see this guy again, but who the hell wants to date a cheap ass?

→ **OPTION #4**

Leave quietly. Just get up without saying a word and leave. He'll get the hint when you don't come back.

OMG Rant!

The Dutch have given the world so much: Rembrandt, Anne Frank's diary, cute little wooden shoes—but why did they have to come up with such a terrible idea as having a woman pay her share? Damn Dutch!

Dating Is No Laughing Matter

Girls, never order a lobster on your date with a boy. For if you order and consume that lobster, the most expensive thing on the menu . . . you have to touch your date's weiner. You have to. It's like a sexual contract from the sea.

—Iliza Shlesinger,
Winner of *Last Comic Standing*

Coffee	A hug
Ice cream/dessert	A kiss
Lunch	A hug and kiss
Drinks	A blow job ('cause you're drunk)
Dinner	Make out with a little groping
Dinner/drinks/dessert	Sex

21. He never, ever disagrees with you

You've always wanted a guy similar to you. One that has a lot of the same interests and beliefs. But not only does this guy think like you, he never contradicts, argues, or denies anything you say. He agrees with everything.

"I don't want to go out tonight, I want to stay in."

"Okay," he replies.

"The sky is green, not blue."

"Yeah, I can see that it is a shade of green. You're right."

"I want you to get a penile implant."

"If that will make you happy."

"I'd rather watch *Project Runway* than the UFC fight you already paid for."

"You know what? Me too. And pay-per-view is only $75 a pop anyway. I'll catch the highlights on *Sports Center* . . . if that's okay with you."

All those yeses make you want to scream NO! Just once, you want to have him challenge you about anything.

→ OPTION #1

Be honest with him. Sit him down and point out the fact that he never disagrees with you about anything and that it's a little weird. Only problem is that he'll probably agree with you which will only make it worse. Damn it!

→ OPTION #2

Use him. See how far you can use this to your advantage. Tell him you think it would be better if he gave you some money so you could buy those hot new shoes you've wanted for a while. And also you think if you get those shoes, he should take you to much nicer restaurants. Also, you think you guys should have an open relationship. If he agrees to all that, you win! Don't worry; when it's time to really end it, he won't disagree.

→ OPTION #3

Do some research. This had to start somewhere, probably with mommy. Find out how their relationship was when he was growing up. If she's the one who did this to him, have a talk with her and maybe she can help out in this situation. Unless she is exactly like her son and agrees with everything you say, then use that weakling too.

OMGjesus!

22. You break your "no sex on the first date" rule

T he date is going great. You are having such a great time— the conversation is easy, the drinks are flowing, and you are feeling that connection so when it comes to that time of the night when you say your goodbyes, you don't. You invite him in, you start fooling around, and then he makes the move. You know that move that says let's make this happen. You have a choice to make here. Have sex on the first date or put the brakes on? Turns out, your brakes are faulty, in fact nonexistent, and the next thing you know, you and him are doing the dirty on your couch while your roommate sleeps a mere ten feet away. Whoops!

→ **OPTION #1**

Enjoy it. As long as he wore a condom, so what if you bumped uglies on the first date? You wanted to, he wanted to (of course), and it was fun. So just let it go, and if he calls again, great, if not, at least you have a juicy story to tell your friends.

→ OPTION #2

Blame it on the alcohol. We all do it, so why not? Keep in mind, however, he will always try to get you drunk from now on. You are on his "booty call" list.

→ OPTION #3

Cry. Girls always use this to get out of uncomfortable situations. Start crying until he either comforts you or leaves. Then call your girlfriends for an emergency therapy session. Don't forget the ice cream!

→ OPTION #4

Pretend it didn't happen. Just act like that didn't happen and when he expects sex on the next date, give him the old, "I'm not that kind of girl!" He'll be totally confused, but that's a good thing. Guys love girls that seem a little crazy. Makes them want us more.

→ OPTION #5

Do it again. Shit, you already did it with this guy so you can keep going without adding to your number. You'll probably be put into the "booty call" category but who cares? He's in yours, too.

In the Future...

If you don't want to have sex on the first date make sure you only have first dates when you have your period. Trust me, if even you still want to have sex, he most likely won't.

23. He's allergic to your cat

In every relationship there comes a time when you have to introduce your new boyfriend to one of the most important people in your life: your cat. Okay, so maybe some would argue that a cat is not a person, but you would strongly disagree. Your cat is your baby and you want your guy to love your baby as much as you. Only one problem: whenever he gets within three feet of your furry baby, he starts sneezing, wheezing, and itching uncontrollably. Your guy is allergic to Fluffy. OMG.

→ **OPTION #1**

Drug him up. It's a known fact that taking allergy medication or getting allergy shots on a regular basis will help reduce the symptoms of the allergy. If he wants you bad enough he will learn to tolerate being a bit overmedicated.

→ **OPTION #2**

Shave your cat. Your guy won't be bothered by Fluffy anymore but you will have one really ugly, unhappy cat.

→ **OPTION #3**

Get rid of the cat. If you love your boyfriend, then there's only one pussy that needs to be taken care of. Say goodbye to Whiskers. It's every girl for herself.

→ OPTION #4

Get rid of the boy. You've been through enough relationships to know that this one probably won't last. That's why you got the cat in the first place, right? Dump him and blame it on the cat. MEOW.

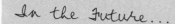

In the Future...

Date a man without an allergy problem. A real man. You think Clint Eastwood would whine like a little bitch because of a cat?

I like my cats the way I like my men, aloof and emotionally unavailable.

24. You don't know when you should have sex

This has always been an issue for you. You start dating someone. You like him and he likes you and the sexual chemistry is definitely there but you're never sure when you should get nude. First date? Third date? One month? Until God takes you aside and tells you? When is the right time to get horizontal?

→ **OPTION #1**

Trust your gut. If you want to bang him on the first date, go ahead. Just be aware that if you sleep with him on the first date, there might not be a second. A lot of guys love the chase as much as the catch.

→ **OPTION #2**

Trust your va-jay-jay. Let your body tell you what it wants. Sure this will probably get you in trouble some of the time, but at least you'll be having fun.

→ **OPTION #3**

Ask him. Tell him you want to wait so at least he'll *think* you are a good girl. If he agrees, if you decide to do it earlier, he'll think that it was because he was so desirable you gave in, not just because you're a horn dog. And if he doesn't, well, he didn't deserve to sleep with you anyway.

Take a poll. Go out on the street and ask fifty random people when they think you should have sex. Sure, this might not help you in deciding when you should do the deed but it will be fun. But since you're not having sex yet you could probably use a little fun right about now.

In the Future...

Be born a guy. Guys never have to worry about this kind of thing.

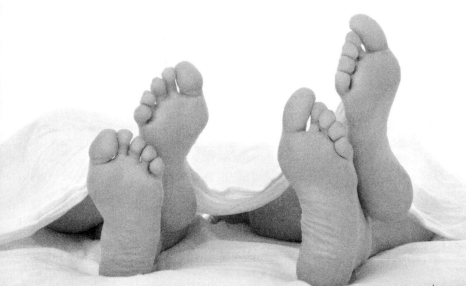

25. You've been on several dates and he hasn't even touched your boobs

On your first date, he gave you a hug and a small kiss on the lips goodnight. *How sweet*, you smile to yourself as you watch him drive away. On the second date, he gave you another long hug and a slightly longer kiss goodnight. *He's so restrained*, you think as you try to push the thought of him taking off your bra with his teeth out of your mind. On the third date, he drops the hug but still leaves you with an irritatingly chaste kiss goodnight. *Talk about being a gentleman* you mutter, now thoroughly frustrated. Now, it's been seven dates and you're *still* just kissing goodnight. What's the deal? Enough with the kiss goodnight!

→ **OPTION #1**

Take the lead. Maybe he is waiting for a sign from you that it's okay to go further. So, grab his ass and shove your tongue down his throat. Subtle, but it might do the trick.

→ **OPTION #2**

Be direct. Ask him what the deal is. He might be involved, or even worse, married. Or worse yet he might have a herpes outbreak at the moment and not want to spread it. Then again, he might just be one of those guys who likes to take it slow. If so, then tell him it's time to hit the gas.

→ OPTION #3

Dump his ass. Being a gentleman is one thing, but apparently this guy has no ambition. Doesn't he want to take it to the next step? He should be trying to climb the corporate ladder—your coop-erate ladder. But no, this guy is happy at the bottom.

OMG in Real Life

I went on like three dates with this guy and he never did anything more than kiss me. We went to his place on the third date, had some drinks, and started kissing. Still, he did nothing. When I put my hand on his leg, he moved it away. I figured he just wasn't into me, you know? I confronted him and he finally came clean. He told me he didn't get turned on by regular stuff like kissing, but that he had a serious foot fetish. At first, I thought it was gross and silly when he got a boner from my stilet-tos, but now I love it. You should see my shoe rack! Filled to the brim.

—Kara

In the Future...

Date a guy with balls. Really, really big ones.

26. He dresses like your uncle (who's blind)

The first time you met him, he was wearing a ripped, pit-stained T-shirt and baggy jeans. The first official date he showed up in a polo shirt two sizes too small and a members only jacket. And the next date he was wearing leather chaps? Okay, you really do like everything about this guy *except* the way he dresses. You keep hoping it will get better but it's getting worse. His closet looks like a rack at Goodwill. OMG, you can't be seen in public with him.

→ **OPTION #1**

Makeover! This is one of the things we ladies do best, we take a "before" and make him an "after." He might resist at first but that is to be expected. Remember, when training an animal, rewards are always given for good behavior. He goes shopping for new clothes with you; you reward him by helping him take them off in the bedroom.

→ **OPTION #2**

Burn baby burn. Start a fire in his closet and blame it on faulty wiring. Now he's forced to buy new clothes.

→ OPTION #3

Take a cue from him. Two can play at this game. Start dressing like a bag lady, with the bags and everything. Of course he might not even notice.

→ OPTION #4

Call in the pros. Hire a fabulous gay guy to come in and just do him over! Snap, some gay men love makeovers even more than women!

→ OPTION #5

Become nudists. Problem solved.

Things You Can't "Fix" on a Guy (No Matter How Hard You Try)

- His penis size
- His height
- His ethnicity
- His overbearing and bitchy mother
- His chronic halitosis

27. His bitchy ex-girlfriend won't stop texting him

As we get older all of us acquire more baggage—AKA, ex-boyfriends and ex-girlfriends. That is to be expected. What is *not* expected is for his ex to constantly still be in contact with him. It's like she has some kind of radar 'cause whenever you guys are together she starts texting him. OMG, why won't that skank stop?

→ **OPTION #1**

Talk to him. He needs to put his foot down, and his phone. He needs to tell his ex that he's dating you now and she has to stop with the texts. Point out that just because she texts him doesn't mean he has to answer. If she doesn't stop, have him change his number—it's clear this psycho isn't going away on her own. If he doesn't agree with you on this, end it. He's obviously not over this text whore.

→ **OPTION #2**

Talk to her. Tell this home wrecker to back off. Remind her that these scenarios never work for the ex. Just look at *Fatal Attraction* and *Obsessed*. It never ends well for the woman who gets in between a happy couple.

→ OPTION #3

Text her. Pretend to be him and send a text from his phone asking her to stop texting. Say something like "It's too painful when you text me, please stop." Girls tend to respond more to a plea than an angry text. So be kind—unless she doesn't stop. Then the gloves can come off.

→ OPTION #4

Read the texts. A women's intuition is never wrong. If you think they might still be seeing each other secretly, the next time you know you have some time alone with his phone (like when he heads to the bathroom with a copy of *ESPN: The Magazine*), snoop away. Maybe he's the one instigating the texts. Find out. Put your mind at ease and your foot up his ass if you catch him doing something wrong.

Guys are like port-o-potties. All the good ones are taken and the bad ones are full of crap. Anonymous

28. You accidentally rip one when you're making out

There's nothing better than a good makeout session. Lips interlocked, hands gliding over each other's bodies. You really like this guy and it seems he is really into you. The kisses are getting hotter and you are definitely feeling it. Then you start feeling something else. What is that pain in your side? Oh shit, it's that gordita burrito you had for lunch. Okay, *slowly* reposition yourself so the gas doesn't . . . too late. You fart—*loudly*. So loudly, in fact, that even his dog looks up at you. OMG, what now?

→ **OPTION #1**

Play dumb. That's right. Act just as surprised as he does. When he looks at you, say, "Oh my God, that wasn't me! Girls don't fart. It must have been the dog! Ew."

→ **OPTION #2**

Think fast. Take your shirt off really fast and show him your boobs. Before he can even comment on that fact that you just caused a sizeable earthquake in the room, he will be staring at boobies. He will soon forget all about the fart—and anything else.

→ OPTION #3

Make a joke. If you can't laugh at yourself, you're in for a lot of embarrassment in your life. Make a joke and don't take yourself so seriously. It will make both of you less embarrassed.

→ OPTION #4

Run. If the embarrassment is too much to take, grab your shit and get the hell out of there.

OMG Rant

Why can't girls get away with farting every once in awhile? Guys are proud when they fart and with the exception of maybe when they're first dating someone, almost *never* get embarrassed. News flash: women fart! Our insides aren't made of cotton candy.

In the Future...

Avoid food that gives you gas on the day of the date, and definitely on the date itself.

Just once, we should be able to let one rip and not pretend it was the dog.

chapter 3

Hooking Up

29. He drools like a bulldog when you make out

You really like this guy. He's funny and sweet and he seems to really like you. Just one problem: he is the worst kisser you have ever been with—and you've had some gems. You keep thinking it will get better, that you can teach him to kiss better, but turns out, you can't. It's like kissing a Saint Bernard. There's drool everywhere and *way* too much tongue. It's almost like he has four tongues. It's hard and fast and at times you can't breathe. OMG, what's the deal with the sloppy kissing?

→ OPTION #1

Be honest. If you really like this guy, tell him he kisses like a big hairy animal. You might want to sweeten that up a bit, but he'll get the point.

→ OPTION #2

Get out now. Kissing is one of the most important things in a relationship and if he's not getting any better you might want to end it now. If this is how he kisses, imagine how he has sex? On second thought, that could be fun.

→ OPTION #3

Gross him out. Start licking, mauling, and drooling all over him and see how he likes it.

→ OPTION #4

Cut off his tongue. Drastic? Maybe. Effective? Definitely. Problem solved. Although he might not want to date you anymore. Just saying.

30. He has more hair on his body than an ape!

You knew he had a great head of hair—that was one of things that attracted you to him in the first place. But what you *didn't* know was that his hair continues down to his chest, around his back, over his ass, and down his legs. He has so much hair that after he takes a shower it looks like a small dog exploded in the bathroom. He sheds more than your cat and when you two are having sex, everything gets caught up in hair. Help!

→ OPTION #1

Wax on, wax off. Take your man to get waxed already. If he argues with you, explain that you're having trouble finding his penis and if he ever wants to have sex again, he needs get things cleaned up a bit. That should do it.

→ OPTION #2

Do it for him. Make it a sexual thing. Light some candles, put on some soft music, and get to waxing, trimming, and shaving him up. It could be hot (or just painful). You might want to throw in a bottle of wine just in case.

→ OPTION #3

Nair it. Replace the body wash in the shower with Nair and let him use it. Then watch the hair just fall off. He might be pissed at first, so quickly throw him on the bed and have your way with him. Tell him you've never been more attracted to him before. Careful, though, make sure it's the body wash and not the shampoo—you'll be stuck with a bald guy who looks like a gorilla from the neck down.

→ OPTION #4

Make animal topiaries. Ya know, like people have in their front yards. They trim their bushes to look like farm animals, dinosaurs, dolphins, anything! Get some shears and trim his pubes, back, and chest. If he doesn't like it, tell him to shave it off.

→ OPTION #5

Pay his friends to do it. Hire his buddies to get him really drunk until he passes out. Then tell them to shave it all off—guys love that kind of crap. His friends can take the blame and you'll have a hairless man.

Win, win!

  He has more hair on his body than an ape!

31. He compares you to his ex in the bedroom

When you start dating someone new, the one thing you never want to hear about is the ex. You know your guy was no virgin when you met, but you don't need to talk about it—especially in the bedroom. Well, not only does your guy bring up his ex, he constantly compares you *to* her in the bedroom. "She used to do this." "She always liked it when I did this." OMG, is this guy for real? If you had known this was a competition, you would've broken out your porn moves, damn it!

→ OPTION #1

Be direct. Tell him this is not okay. Not only do you not want to hear about his ex-girlfriend all the time, you definitely do not want to be compared to her in the bedroom. If he apologizes and seems genuinely sincere, give it another try. If he gets defensive, get out fast. This can only get worse.

→ OPTION #2

Invite his ex to join. Apparently, he hasn't gotten over this bitch so invite her to join or at least watch, then she can tell you firsthand what it is you're doing incorrectly. Oh yeah, then dump that asshole—and go out for drinks with your new friend.

→ OPTION #3

Turn the tables on him. Start talking about *your* ex in the bedroom. Better yet, bring in a tape of the two of you having sex and point out all the things you liked him to do. That should shut him up.

→ OPTION #4

Be open. Maybe his ex truly is amazing in the sack. So have sex with your guy, tape it, and send it to his ex for some feedback. Maybe she's got some wicked moves.

→ OPTION #5

Rock his world. Time to break out the big guns. Do a little research and pick up some new moves. The next time you have sex, you will blow his mind. Right after his mind-blowing orgasm, turn to him and say, "I bet your ex never did that!"

Things You Should Do During Sex

- Use sex toys with your partner
- Record it
- Role play
- Drugs

Thing You Shouldn't Do During Sex

- Cry
- Read a book
- Bleed profusely from nose
- Cause bodily harm (unless he asks you to)

In the Future...

Date a virgin. Then he has nothing to compare you to!

32. He "forgot" to tell you he has crabs!

Everything is going great. You really like him, and he seems to like you. He's funny, caring, and giving. *Really* giving. In fact, he's given you something you don't remember asking for: crabs. That's right, you've only slept together once but that's all it takes for these creepy crawlers to set up shop. Now you're itching, scratching, and picking at yourself like a rabid dog.

→ STEP #1

Confront him! Explain to this dirty pig that when you went to bed with him you thought it was just the two of you, not thousands of tiny crabs.

→ STEP #2

Get treatment. Go to a public lice specialist and get rid of these little buggers! Then burn your sheets!

Men Are No Laughing Matter

"Men are liars. We lie about lying if we have to." —Jay Leno

→ STEP #3

Get even. Make sure his friends and future girlfriends know what happened. Post it on Facebook. When he confronts you about it tell him, "Oops, I 'forgot' I did that."

In the Future . . .

Inspect your man before sex. Do a little marine life expedition and make sure for yourself. If you spot something moving in his pubes, run!

33. You wake in a puddle of your boyfriend's piss, again!

There's nothing better than waking up in the morning with your boyfriend next to you. No more walk of shame after a hot night of sex. Your boyfriend and you have gotten to that comfortable place of spending the night. But it looks like your boyfriend has gotten a little too comfortable. As you lie in bed, you notice the sheets are wet. OMG, did I get my period? Did I spill water in the bed? Then you look down and suddenly it hits you. The smell, anyway. Someone pissed the bed, and it wasn't you. Maybe your guy was too drunk to get up. Maybe he was too lazy. It doesn't really matter the reason. Your boyfriend has pissed the bed again and you have had enough.

→ **OPTION #1**

Rub his face in it. Grab him by the collar and shove his face in his pee pee mess, just like when a dog pees on the rug. If he is as smart as a puppy, he'll learn his lesson soon.

→ **OPTION #2**

Buy him diapers. If this only happens when he has a little too much to drink, then get him some big boy pull-ups to wear before you go to bed. If he complains, get him superhero pull-ups. Little boys love superheroes, maybe big boys do, too!

→ OPTION #3

Get rubber sheets. Uncomfortable and not very sexy, but much easier to clean.

→ OPTION #4

Put him in the dog house. Literally. If he is going to act like an animal, then that's how he is going to be treated.

→ OPTION #5

Put him to sleep. There is just no training some animals. You've tried all you can, but it's time to face the music and take him to the pound. He is out of control and, for the sake of humanity, he must be put down.

→ OPTION #6

Keep a bucket next to the bed. Let him piss in that if he really can't make it to the bathroom. Keep one on your side of the bed in case you need to vomit from the thought of a piss bucket in your bedroom.

OMGjesus!

34. He's way too small

You know what they say: "It's not the size of the package; it's what's inside that counts." You know what's inside of your boyfriend's small penis? A small penis. You love everything about your guy except that it looks like he stopped growing down there sometime in middle school, not that you've ever had sex with a teenager—at least since you've been a teenager. You know that size shouldn't matter, but if you can't feel it, what's the point?

→ **OPTION #1**

Pump it up. Buy him the penis pump. Maybe tell him it's just a sex toy so he doesn't feel bad. Then pump that shit up.

→ **OPTION #2**

Tighten your hoo-ha. Try some Kegels to make sure you're in top form down there. Start right now, no one's looking.

→ **OPTION #3**

Live with it. If you love him, you should be able to live with this. If it feels good for him, great. When he's done, just have him take care of you in others ways. Unless he has a really small tongue, too; then you're screwed.

→ **OPTION #4**

Get a replacement. Buy yourself a vibrator and use that for a while. It's not cheating and now you'll both be satisfied.

→ **OPTION #5**

Put it somewhere smaller, like your ear.

35. He falls asleep while giving you oral sex

There he goes. "Down South" as you and your girlfriends like to call it. This feels pretty good. You just lay back, relax, and let him give you pleasure. You really start getting into it when things start to slow down and then . . . hello? What happened? You sit up and notice that not only has your guy stopped doing what he was doing, he fell asleep on the job!

→ OPTION #1

Wake his ass up. Squeeze your legs together on his head and gently remind him that he has not yet finished his job. He should snap right back up. Kinda like when you doze off for a second while driving. Tell him to keep his eyes on the road.

→ OPTION #2

Finish the job yourself. Kick him out of the bed and take care of business. Damn, a girl's work is never done.

→ OPTION #3

Use some caffeinated lotion down there, so while he's doing the deed he can get a little pick-me-up. Hey, this could be big. Market that shit and make millions. Then dump this loser and buy yourself a hotter, younger guy who knows how to stay awake during those intimate moments.

OMG in Real Life

Some guys love getting really creative with oral sex. I once had a guy decide he was going to do the alphabet with his tongue. I was like screw the alphabet, just dot the I, dot the I, dot the I. . . .

In the Future...

Date an insomniac with a cunnilingus fetish. He'll be down there for days.

36. He calls you "Christy" during sex . . . your name is Kim

Remember the first time your partner spoke in the bedroom? It was weird, right? When you start having sex with a new partner, you're both concentrating, so there is no talking. But then you both get good at it and you start with the sex talk. You know, the "Ohh yeah, right there," and the standby "You like that huh?" and "That's it right there, DON'T move." And even better is when your guy calls out your name. "Christy! Christy! Christy!" Except your name is Kim! OMG did he just call you by the wrong name in the sack?!

→ **OPTION #1**

Stop short. That's right, just before he's about to finish, push him off you and onto the floor. Unless you're already on the floor then just push him off you. Then tell him calmly, "I'm sure Christy would have let you finish if she were here. But Janis thinks you're an asshole and you can go f*#k yourself."

→ **OPTION #2**

Flip the switch. Call him by another name. Screw it. Call him by *several* names. That should throw him for sure. "Yeah, that's it Mike, give it to me. Come on, Steven. You know how I like it, Bill. I love it when you do that, Trevor. You are the best lover, Dick."

→ OPTION #3

Start crying. Why not? It's our birthright to break into tears whenever we want. He might think you're crying because the sex is so good. Yeah right, like that would ever happen!

→ OPTION #4

Finish. The sex and the relationship. Keep going, make sure he takes care of you, whatever your name is, then dump his ass.

→ OPTION #5

Change your name. Hey, you might look like a Christy, ever think of that? Maybe that's how he sees you. And hey there are a lot of hot women named Christy out there—Christie Brinkley, Christy Turlington, Agatha Christie. Okay maybe not that last one but you get the point. You go, Christy!

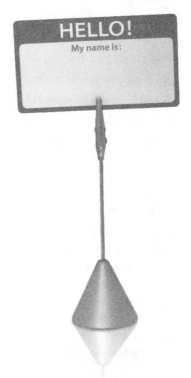

37. He's a bit "premature"

The first time it happened, you assumed it was because he was a little nervous. The second time, you assumed it was because he was a little drunk, but now it seems it happens all the time. In fact the last time, he finished before you even got your bra off. There are some things in life we like coming early. Birthday presents, tax returns, paychecks, but as far as your boyfriend coming too early, that's not so good.

→ **OPTION #1**

Build up his tolerance. You might have to have sex half a dozen times in one day but at least by the third time in as many hours he should be able to last longer. You, however, could have problems walking the next day.

→ **OPTION #2**

Talk nondirty. While doing the deed, whisper not so hot things to your man. Men are very visual so paint a not so pretty picture in his mind to make him last longer. Like, "You love watching naked old people playing vollyball," "dead puppies," or just talk about your feelings. That should kill the mood.

→ OPTION #3

Encourage porn. Before you guys get together, tell him to watch a little porn and take care of business so he won't show up with a loaded gun. Kinda of the same theory as Option #1, but without putting you in as much pain.

→ OPTION #4

Get him on antidepressants. Most antidepressants like Prozac have the side effect of making it very difficult for a man to have an orgasm which is a good thing for your man. Not to mention, it must be depressing to suck in bed.

→ OPTION #5

Scream. That's right, just before he is about to let loose, scream bloody murder. This will scare the shit out of him and stop the orgasm. You will probably end up scarring him for life, but so be it.

In the Future...

Date an old man. They can barely get it up, let alone come too soon. True, old men are, well, old—but between premature and overly mature, it's better to take the latter.

38. He's way too kinky for you

You've always considered yourself someone who likes to try new things. Like the first time you tried sushi, or went bungee jumping. So when your boyfriend suggested that you spice things up in the bedroom, you were all for it. Maybe some fuzzy handcuffs, a blindfold, or even an edible lube. But when you find yourself in head to toe leather and your boyfriend is wearing a dog collar and wants you to lead him around on all fours, you know you've crossed the line from spicy to freaky. Now he wants to give you a golden shower—OMG, stop!

→ **OPTION #1**

Have a safe word. Look, some of this stuff can be fun and if you guys trust each other, why not? But have a safe word so he knows when it's gone too far. My safe word is STOP THAT CRAZY SHIT, ASSHOLE. That always works for me.

Men are like a fine wine. They all start out like grapes, and it's our job to stomp on them and keep them in the dark until they mature into something you'd like to have dinner with.

Kathleen Mifsud

→ **OPTION #2**

Just say no. If this is just not your style, then politely decline. This might end your relationship but then you are free to go find someone who is just as boring as you in the bedroom.

→ **OPTION #3**

Crank it up a notch. He's likes it kinky? Give him kinky. Really kinky. Make sushi on his naked body. Pour hot wax on his nipples. Chain him up naked and invite friends to come over and pet the animal. This should freak him out enough to dial it down a little.

Or, he might like it. Then the joke's on you.

39. Your boyfriend is a sleepwalker

You *finally* have a boyfriend. One who likes spending the night at your place. One who even likes to spoon with you. Although, the spooning doesn't last as long as you would like. Lately, you noticed he's been getting up a lot in the middle of the night. What's the deal? He must have a very small bladder. One night, he accidentally wakes you up getting out of bed and you ask him if everything is alright. He doesn't answer so you get up and follow him . . . watch in amazement as he opens the fridge and starts rummaging through it. You call his name, and he turns and looks at you like he's never seen you before. He then walks out of your place and starts heading down the street, naked! OMG, he's totally sleepwalking.

→ **OPTION #1**

Get professional help. Most of the time a doctor can get to the bottom of why this is happening. Maybe it only happens when he's stressed. Whatever the case let the experts deal with it, unless you're a doctor. Then help him, but also charge him.

→ **OPTION #2**

Tape him. The next time it happens, grab your camera and start filming. Then post it on YouTube and make him an Internet sensation. Sure he'll be embarrassed, but he might become famous and then you'll be the girlfriend of a pseudo-celebrity. Score!

OMG Fact

You should never wake up a sleep-walker. Unless you catch him pee-ing in the refrigerator, then throw a large object at him, 'cause that's just gross.

→ OPTION #3

Tie him down. If you're worried that something might happen then make sure he can't get anywhere. Although, if he has to pee then you're screwed. So maybe tie a bag to his ding dong for that.

→ OPTION #4

Lock the doors. If Option #3 seems a little too extreme, just lock the doors from the inside. Again, if you don't have a bath-room in your room this can be a messy situation. In that case, just use a bucket and make him empty it in the morning.

>>> 40. He barks like a dog and makes weird faces during sex

Remember your mom's favorite old saying, "Don't make faces or one day your face will get stuck like that"? Well, I guess your boyfriend never heard that 'cause he makes some really weird faces during sex. And not just faces—sometimes he sounds like a guinea pig in heat. He squeals and groans and has a strange look like he smells something awful. It's distracting to say the least. What to do when your guy kills the mood?

→ OPTION #1

Close your eyes, and ears. Keep your eyes shut no matter what. Tape them closed if you have to, and stick those foam earplugs in as well—that way you can't hear the calls of the wild. Once you have blocked out all things distracting, imagine someone else, someone hotter who doesn't makes faces or strange sounds. This could actually be fun, 'cause it will force you to use your other senses, like your sense of touch.

→ OPTION #2

Put a bag over his head. Tell him this is something you're really into, which is a little weird but that's just how you roll. If he wants to make you happy, he'll do it. Paint a cute face on the bag while you're at.

→ OPTION #3

Drown him out. Start moaning and groaning louder than him. As for the faces, that should stop when he realizes you're screaming during sex. Your neighbors might get pissed, but one problem at a time.

→ OPTION #4

Make a sex tape. Then show it to him and see if he notices the way he is contorting his face and the crazy wildebeest sounds he's making. He'll probably be so embarrassed he will try to be more aware of it in the future. If he's not, then post it online and let him read the comments. That should do it!

OMG in Real Life

I had this boyfriend who, right as he was climaxing, would roll his eyes back in his head. The first time he did it, I freaked out. I thought he was having a stroke or something. He said he didn't realize he was doing it, but it was creepy. I mean all I could see was the whites of his eyes. I eventually broke up with him, not about that but to be honest it helped me make that decision.

—Elle

In the Future...

Date a mute with a trust fund and a five-pound penis. You won't hear a peep out of him, but you'll be screaming like a hyena.

>>>> 41. You find out he's slept with over 116 chicks

You knew your boyfriend wasn't a virgin when you met him. You also knew there would be a time in the relationship when you would have to reveal the "number" (the number of sexual partners you've both had before you started dating). It's a sick curiosity we human beings have. So when it comes time to make your list it's not very hard, or long. Just that loser you lost your virginity to after homecoming weekend, your douche bag ex-boyfriend, and a couple of random guys you used to get over that douche bag. You expect that his number will be a little higher of course but when he tells you the number you're shocked. "Uhh . . . 115, no, you're 116." OMG! WHAT?! You try to laugh it off, he can't be serious, but he is. He has slept with more than 100 different women. Now what?

→ OPTION #1

Get tested immediately. If he's been with that many women, odds are he might have something. Get tested for everything and make sure he wears a condom every time until you know he's clean. Shit, make him wear two condoms.

→ OPTION #2

Get him tested. Now you know your bill of health, make sure he is up to code. If he tries to tell you he doesn't need to be tested, cut off his dick. Just kidding, but that is a deal breaker. Proceed to Option #3.

→ OPTION #3

Break up. Even if you are both clean, you might have a problem getting past that high number of his. Wondering if you're as good in the bedroom as just one of his exes can drive you nuts. Now think about all 100 of them! That will drive you to drink.

→ OPTION #4

Let it go. If Option 3 is too drastic and you're confident in your relationship and abilities in the bedroom, then let it go. But remember if you say you're fine with it, you really better be fine with it. Don't keep bringing it up every time you two have an argument.

Sex Is No Laughing Matter

"Women might be able to fake orgasms. But men can fake a whole relationship."
—Sharon Stone

→ OPTION #5

Start screwing. That's right, spread your legs and start raising that number of yours. You're not gonna let this guy beat you, are you? You will have to change your name to SLUT, but that's cool . . . looks great on a T-shirt.

OMGesus!

42. He's really hung!

You're just about to do the deed for the first time and he asks you, "Okay, are you ready?" *Well, hell, dude, I'm naked and lying underneath you. What the hell else am I doing here?* you think to yourself. But instead you say, "yes."

"Here it comes."

"Oh yeah, there it is," you say.

Then, um, it doesn't feel good. In fact, that hurts. Maybe you should shift positions. Nope, that still hurts—a lot. Wow, you knew he was well endowed, but this is ridiculous. Is that even possible? You keep trying to hide the fact that it really doesn't feel good when he moves and . . . ouch! OMG! Damn, this guy is hung like a horse.

→ STEP #1

Warm up. Okay, you can do this. Before you guys have sex, start stretching out, doing squats, and so on. Maybe take a warm bath and do some breathing exercises. Get yourself mentally ready for the game.

→ STEP #2

Lube up. Break out the lube and grease that sucker up. That should help.

→ STEP #3

Get comfortable. This one is important. Since he's enormous, the truth is there will be only a few positions that will work for you. Sideways could work, maybe you on top, that way you have the control. No doggie style—you'll end up getting pinned down and that is not comfortable.

→ STEP #4

Try to enjoy it. Hopefully you'll soon start to enjoy what most men wish they had. Then the more you get used to it, the better it will feel and the more fun you guys will have. But remember if you do get used to it, your next guy may be a total letdown. Ugh.

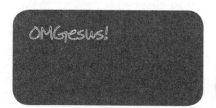

OMGjesus!

How to Spot a Guy with a Small Penis

He is driving a truck with giant wheels.

OMG Fact

Featured in a HBO documentary and *Rolling Stone*, Jonah Falcon has the record for the world's largest penis at a staggering 13.5 inches. And guess what? He's 39 years old, unemployed, and living with his mother (according to *The Huffington Post*). So hey, God giveth and God taketh away!

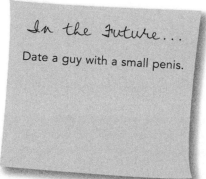

In the Future...

Date a guy with a small penis.

43. He never goes down on you

Relationships are about give and take. Compromising and making your partner happy. You do his laundry, he takes out the trash. You cook him dinner, he changes the oil in your car. You give him a BJ, he says thank you. Wait a second, what's the deal here? Turns out in all the time you've been together, he has yet to go Down South. Whenever you suddenly give him hints, like the nudge to move a little lower, he doesn't seem to catch on or he does but is just outright ignoring you. Either way, this give and receive thing is bullshit—you're giving but NOT receiving.

→ OPTION #1

Stop being subtle. The nudge is apparently not getting the job done here so be a little more aggressive. Shit, be a lot more aggressive. Stand over him naked and scream, "Come and get it!"

→ OPTION #2

Stop giving. Look, it's a two-way street and if one way is closed for construction then close your side, too. He'll try to get you back with his own subtle hints, but don't give in. The boy needs to be taught a lesson.

→ OPTION #3

Conversate. If you're not one to play games then just sit him down and get to the bottom of it. Maybe he's scared to do it, 'cause he thinks he's not good at it or maybe he's never done it and has no clue what to do. The fact is you'll never know if you don't ask. If he needs some instructions then by all means, school him.

OMG Fact

According to Random Facts.com, women who went to college are more likely to enjoy receiving and giving oral sex. Trust me, you don't need a degree to enjoy it.

OMG Rant:
What's with the Nudge?

We all know the nudge, right? Guys love to gently push our heads down in that general direction when they want us to you know . . . anyway, enough! We know where "it" is, no need to push us down there. It's not like any girl has ever said, "Oh *that's* where your penis is, thank God you nudged me in that direction. I thought it was behind your ear!" Stop it, already. We will get there when we get there, and if we want to get there! After all, women don't do that; we assume you will also get there in due time. Having said that, just once I wish we would take control and steer them where we want them to go. Give 'em a giant nudge. It would make things a lot easier.

chapter 4

OMG, You're BF/GF

44. He forgot your birthday

Your mom was the first call of the day, your dad the second. Grandparents after that. Your BFF called to see where the party was. You have over fifty "HAPPY BIRTHDAYS" on your Facebook profile page, some from people you haven't heard from in years. Even your weirdo boss sent you an awkward e-card. Seems everyone has remembered your B-day, except, oh yeah—your boyfriend. You keep thinking he's not bringing it up on purpose. Like he's planning a surprise something for you. But the later in the day it gets, it's obvious, this dude has really just forgotten. What a dumbass!

→ **OPTION #1**

Kill him with kindness. Trust me, this will send his guilt way over the edge. Start out by saying, "It's okay that you forgot my birthday today." Then go with things like, "It's alright; I know you have other really big things going on in your head." Or, "It's just a birthday, no big deal." This will drive him crazy trying to figure out why you're not upset at all.

→ **OPTION #2**

Kill him. Okay, not literally, but let loose with some rage on his ass. In this day and age there's no excuse for him to forget a birthday. With Facebook, Twitter, MySpace, and BirthdayAlarm.com, no one can *ever* say they forgot anyone's birthday.

→ OPTION #3

Guilt him. Not just today, not just tomorrow, but every day and for the rest of his life. The ammunition you gain from him forgetting your birthday is the real gift that will keep on giving. In the long run, this ammo beats a Snuggie any day.

→ OPTION #4

Let it go. Sure it sucks, but it happens. If he seems genuinely sorry, then forgive him and let him make it up to you with really expensive shoes. If he doesn't seem genuinely sorry, buy yourself the really expensive shoes for your birthday and kick him in the face.

→ OPTION #5

Convert to Jehovah's Witness—they don't celebrate birthdays at all. Nor do they celebrate most holidays. This way you won't be let down when your man forgets Valentine's Day too.

→ OPTION #6

Get revenge. Pretend to accept his desperate apology and turn your efforts and thoughts to revenge. Wait until the day he really needs you—like a critical speech at a conference he is giving or when he goes into the hospital for an emergency lung transplant. Then, don't show up to show support. That'll teach him.

OMG Rant

Okay, here's my problem. Why do women make such a big deal about their birthdays, yet lie about their age? We're supposed to be *celebrating* the fact that we were born into this world and the fact that we are proud of how good we look at any age. If you expect your guy to make a big hoopla every year on your birthday, then you better stop lying about the year you were born. Trust me; he'll start to catch on. And if you worry about getting older and still being able to attract and keep young, cute guys—don't. Haven't you heard? Cougars are very trendy right now—here's hoping they're still trendy when you're old enough to be one.

45. You get an amazing new haircut and he doesn't notice

There's nothing better than a great haircut. It can change your whole day. You know that feeling—you want to go everywhere and show it off. You have a bounce in your step. You're glowing. You can't *wait* for your boyfriend to see you. You just know he'll be so blown away by this new 'do, he'll pick you up in his arms and carry you off into the bedroom, then take you out to an amazing dinner where he can show you off to everyone before heading back to the bedroom. Yes, what a day this will be. You open the door, he walks in, and . . . nothing. He says *nothing*! He doesn't even notice. How the f#@* can that be?

→ OPTION #1

Give him some hints. Some guys are just clueless and they need a little push. Ask him if he notices anything different about you. Or ask your sister to compliment your new 'do right in front of the idiot's face. If he still doesn't get it, break up; he's a moron who is obviously only fixated on himself.

→ OPTION #2

Shave it all off. He obviously doesn't care what you look like so why have hair at all? We all know what a pain it is. Think about all the time you'll save by not having to do your hair every day, and all the money you'll save not buying those ridiculously priced hair care products. Shave it sister; make a statement for all women!

→ OPTION #3

Do nothing. Who cares if he doesn't notice? It's how you feel about yourself that matters, right?

Ha! Who am I kidding? Dump this asshole and go out with your sexy new 'do and "do" someone else!

If truth is beauty, how come no one has their hair done in a library?
Lily Tomlin

46. He doesn't have a car and you're sick of driving his sorry ass around

When you first started dating, you thought it was kinda cute that he didn't have a car. He's environmentally conscious—how sweet. He walks, takes the bus, and rides his bike. He cares about the earth and his health. So you didn't really mind driving him to dinner and the movies and over to his place. But lately, instead of "Want to go there?" it's "Can you take me here?" "Can you take me there?" "I need to buy this, pick up that, and visit him." OMG, are you his freaking chauffeur?! And the worst part is he hasn't *once* offered to pay for gas. Turns out his not having a car is not so frickin' cute after all.

→ **OPTION #1**

Put the brakes on. We're only treated the way we let others treat us. It's not his fault if you keep on driving him around. If he needs to go somewhere, tell him to take the bus. Or better yet, buy a car. Sure, it's nice to want to save the environment—but not at your expense.

→ OPTION #2

Let him take the wheel. Okay, so maybe he can't afford to buy a car, then let him drive yours. Unless you need it, then he can chauffeur you around for a change, *then* go do what he needs to. But make sure he does chip in for gas. But God bless that motherf#@*er if he puts a dent in your wheels.

→ OPTION #3

Get rid of your car. You can't drive him around if you don't have a car. Now you're both screwed but at least you still have each other. Unless he was just using you for your car, which means you are really screwed and *not* in the good way.

→ OPTION #4

Get rid of your boyfriend. You can't drive him around if you're not dating him anymore. I mean, you can but that would just make you really pathetic.

In the Future...

Live in a place where no one needs a car like NYC, London, or a tribal outpost deep in the Amazon.

Match the Ride to the Guy

1. Ford Bronco

2. Mercedes

3. Smart Car

4. Bentley

5. Mustang

6. Porsche convertible

7. Beat-up Camry

A. Lawyer

B. In the closet

C. Sugar Daddy

D. Blue collar

E. Just got his license

F. Big fan of *The Jersey Shore*

G. Trust fund baby

Answers: 1/D, 2/A, 3/B, 4/C, 5/F, 6/G, 7/E

He doesn't have a car and you're sick of driving his sorry ass around **< OMG!** Guys | 97

47. He's OCD neat and thinks you're a slob

H is car is spotless—even after a cross-country road trip. His shirts are always pressed—even his T-shirts. His apartment is immaculate—and he makes you fold your pajamas, even if you're whipping them off to attack him. This is different; most guys you date live like, well, ya know—guys. But not this one. He is clean—very clean. In fact, the more you get to know him, the more you've started to notice that this might be a problem. And now his problem is becoming *your* problem because he's constantly make little comments about how your place isn't as clean as it should be. You're not a clean freak but you're not a total pig either. Your boyfriend, on the other hand, disagrees—and won't STFU about it.

→ OPTION #1

Use it. If he likes to clean so much, put him to work. Let him clean your apartment, your car, and whatever else you need cleaning. This could be the best thing for you: a boyfriend and a maid wrapped up in one. Win, win.

→ OPTION #2

Get him help. This might be bordering on a more serious problem: Obsessive Compulsive Douche Bag Syndrome (or OCDBS). This might be the perfect time to hook him up with the therapist so he can work this shit out. And hey—OCD is very trendy right now.

→ OPTION #3

Flip the switch. He thinks you're a slob now, just wait. Start trashing his place and his car and watch him explode, just like your relationship.

→ OPTION #4

Join in. Hey, there are worse things in life to being a total neat freak. Follow his lead and start cleaning everything. Then the two of you can really feed off each other's OCD and be miserable—but squeaky clean—together.

Does Your Guy Have OCDBS?

Does he . . .

- Wash his hands extensively?
- Take more than three showers a day?
- Walk around with a can of Lysol?
- Wear rubber gloves when he masturbates?
- Wear rubber gloves when *you* masturbate?

48. You plan a surprise party for him and he never shows

You've been planning this for a month. You got all his friends' contact info from his roommate, you set up the perfect lie about a "quiet night at your place" so he'll have no idea you're planning this party, and everyone has been playing along so well. So the night arrives and you're all waiting patiently for his car to drive up. Everyone is in their hiding place ready to go. An hour goes by with three false alarms. Then another hour, then another, and people are starting to get restless—and drunk. So you break down and call your guy to see where he's at. Turns out, that bastard blew you off and took off for the weekend spontaneously—leaving you with a house full of *his* friends. OMG, he's not coming to his own party, what now?!

→ OPTION #1

Have fun. So what if the guest of honor never showed and you're left with the humiliation of fifty people knowing your boyfriend stood you up. There are people, there's food, and there's booze—sounds like fun to me. Laugh it off and party it up. You can deal with the rest tomorrow when you're hungover. That will make everything better.

→ OPTION #2

Tell him. Even though he didn't know there was gonna be a party, he doesn't have the right to just split without even mentioning it to you. If he had told you he was thinking of leaving town for the night, you would have stopped him. The fact is, you put all this hard work into doing something special for him and damn it, he needs to know! The guilt should drive him to come right back home and make it up to you.

→ OPTION #3

Bring the party to him. Pack everyone in the car and just show up where he's at. SURPRISE!! Careful though, when guys take off without telling their girlfriends there's a chance they may be cheating. Catch him with another girl and the surprise will *definitely* be on you.

OMG in Real Life

I once planned a surprise party for my boyfriend. I hadn't eaten at all that day and I was so nervous about everything going off just right that I accidentally got really drunk before he even got there. Finally, we hear him coming. Everyone hides except me, because I could barely walk, let alone hide. My boyfriend comes in, everyone jumps up and screams "SURPRISE!" and he turns to me just as I puke all over the floor. It was really gross, but perfectly timed. That was the last surprise party I ever planned.

—Amy

In the Future...

Don't date the type of asshole who blows off his girlfriend without a second thought.

49. He doesn't believe in Valentine's Day

You can't wait to celebrate your first Valentine's Day with your new boyfriend. It's been a couple years since you were lucky enough to have a boyfriend on Valentine's Day, especially one who you liked so much. Where is he going to take you? What is he going to give you? OMG, you are so excited you could just scream. Then, you find out that you aren't going anywhere, and you aren't getting anything. Why? Because he doesn't "believe" in Valentine's Day. O-M-F'ing-G!

→ **OPTION #1**

Share your "beliefs" with him. Two can play at that game. Tell him that if he doesn't believe in Valentine's Day, you no longer believe in blow jobs. We'll see how long it takes him to make reservations somewhere nice after that.

→ **OPTION #2**

Break up. Right away. Don't even talk about it. Being with a man is good for three things: sex, fixing stuff, and the prospect of being taken out on Valentine's Day. Dump him.

→ OPTION #3

Give him a Valentine's Day he'll never forget. He might not want to make yours very special, but that doesn't mean you can't make his unforgettable. Read up on the Valentine's Day massacre in the Prohibition Era, the famous incident in which Al Capone's men dressed as cops murdered over ten rival mobsters. Study how they did it, and then kill your boyfriend.

→ OPTION #4

Get over it. Valentine's Day is a fake holiday that the card and candy industry has glorified. Just be happy you have a boyfriend who seems to really care about you and quit your bitching. If you can't get over it, send him my way—I'll make him happy.

50. His place looks like he is auditioning for *Hoarders*

Guys: they're known for being, well, pigs. They never put anything anyway; they will wear the same pair of jeans until they can walk on their own; and if you don't remind them to shower once in awhile they would never do it. We as girls expect this. So the first time you actually saw your boyfriend's place you weren't that shocked. It was bad but you assumed this was just a bad day, ya know, before he cleans. Turns out this was a good day. He actually straightened the place up before you got there. OMG, your guy is a freakin' slob. There is spaghetti on the floor. Empty pizza boxes and cans of beer everywhere. You'd rather pop a squat in the backyard than sit on his toilet. A new life form is taking over the fridge and what the hell is growing in his closet?!

→ **OPTION #1**

Never go back. Okay, so he is a total and utter piggy. That's fine, just never go back to that hell hole. Always insist he come to your place. And if you ever do go back there for any reason, make sure you get your shots and don the cutest Hazmat suit you can find.

→ OPTION #2

Stage an intervention—with his mom in tow. Surprise him one day by showing up with his mother. When she sees the way her little boy is living she will either scold him or clean the place herself. Either way this should get the job done.

→ OPTION #3

Call the landlord. Anonymously of course, but most places won't allow their tenants to keep their home in this state of uncleanliness. He will be forced to clean. Watch out, though—you may end up with a piggy new roommate if his landlord evicts him.

→ OPTION #4

Enjoy it. Hey, it might be fun living like this. Not having to clean up after yourself could be very liberating, so try it for a while. Stop showering; leave half eaten shit anywhere you want. Use the toilet and don't flush. Grow fun new life forms of your own. You'll probably lose most of your friends and gain a few infections, but at least you and your equally dirty boyfriend will have each other.

→ OPTION #5

Call in the pros. Get one of those shows like *Clean House* to come and, well, clean house. Then you can proudly brag to your friends and family, "That's my dirty gross boyfriend on TV."

Notorious Celebrity Slobs (According to ABC News Entertainment Online)

- Kevin Federline (Are we surprised?)
- Lindsey Lohan (She's has no time to clean, she's using that time to get wasted)
- Beyoncé (Looks like she got more than just junk in her trunk)
- Charlize Theron (We'll give her a pass, cause she's so beautiful)

51. He is constantly keeping tabs on you

You love that your guy takes an interest in your day. So thoughtful. He'll send you a text on your way to work to let you know he's thinking of you. Then later he'll call, then send another text "just to check in." He calls and texts a lot. Like really a lot. And now it seems more like he's keeping tabs on what you're doing. What's next, a GPS system in your purse? ENOUGH!

→ OPTION #1

Take him along. He wants to know where you are throughout the day, take him. Take him to yoga class, coffee with the girls, and then to your gynecologist appointment. Make him come in just so he really knows what's going on in there. Then have him come with you while you listen to your BFF cry about her latest boy problems. This one day should be enough to loosen the reins on you.

→ OPTION #2

Start keeping tabs on him. Call him every twenty minutes "just to check in." Show up at his work. Stop by his softball practice. Drive by the gas station as he's getting gas. This should scare the shit out of him enough to back off. Careful though, he might end up getting a restraining order on you.

→ OPTION #3

Don't answer. When he calls or texts, you tell him you're busy and you'll talk to him later—then stop answering his calls and texts. If he comes to find out what you're doing, get a restraining order on *him*.

→ OPTION #4

Get him a life. Maybe he's keeping tabs on you 'cause he's bored. Find him a hobby other than you. Maybe kite flying, painting, or collecting stamps. Although then you have a new problem. Do you really want to date a stamp collector?

An Hour in the Life of a Stalker (er, Attentive Boyfriend)

9:15 a.m. Good morn!

9:17 a.m. Miss you.

9:22 a.m. On ur way to work?

9:30 a.m. See you 2night?

9:32 a.m. R u there?

9:33 a.m. Where u at?

9:36 a.m. R u @ work?

9:37 a.m. Hello?

9:38 a.m. R u ok?

9:45 a.m. OMG R u ok?

10 a.m. answer me!

10:02 a.m. R u breaking up with me?

10:03 a.m. It's like that?

10:04 a.m. u r making a HUGE mistake

10:10 a.m. is it Tom? R u leaving me for ur pig boss?

10:15 a.m. I am going 2 kill him and u if u don't answer me!

10:16 a.m. Say ur prayers! LOL. Have fun w/him in hell!!!

10:30 a.m. I am sorry. Movie tonite?

>> 52. You want to go to wine country— he takes you to NASCAR

It's no secret that men and women are different. We ladies like the finer things in life like good wine, nice clothes, and dinner by candlelight. Most men, on the other hand, would prefer buffalo wings, beer, and watching other dumb men drive a car really, really fast around a circle. NASCAR, one of the least interesting things to witness in the world, is where he takes you on vacation?! What about touring wine country? OMG, this vacation sucks!

→ OPTION #1

Steal a stock car . . . and leave town. Time that you went out on your own and sought adventure. You don't need a man to have fun. Dub yourself Thelma and find your Louise, then put the pedal to the metal and fly like the wind—but consider heading to Napa rather than over a cliff.

→ OPTION #2

Steal a stock car . . . and run him over. Hey, any man that thinks watching cars go around a track 400 times is entertaining obviously needs some real excitement. Give it to him.

→ OPTION #3

If you can't beat 'em . . . might as well just try to make the most of it. Cut the sleeves off of your jean shirt, rip your jeans up, grab a can of Bud, and live it up! Your guy will appreciate the effort. But make sure he knows that he owes you big next time. Think Paris, baby!

Wine country	Pretentious
Camping	Adventurous
Going on a cruise	Lazy (and fat, once you get back. They'll stuff you full of crap on a cruise.)
Florida	Old
Death Valley	Dying
Cancun	Drunk
Hedonism	Slutty

53. Your boyfriend is tagged in some random skank's Facebook profile pic

It's just another day. You get breakfast, go to work, and sit down to your computer in your cubicle for another grueling day of pretending to work while staring at your Facebook page. But then you notice something. You boyfriend has a new "friend." That's right, a hot chick who you have never seen before. You check out her page. Hmm, interesting. A picture of her and him at the beach. When was that taken? Must be recent. "Friend," eh? Sonofabitch!

→ **OPTION #1**

Attack. Think later, attack now. Send her a message asking her how the hell she knows your man and if she knows that you are his girlfriend.

→ **OPTION #2**

Go for the sneak attack; it's better than blowing up. After all maybe he has been having an affair with her for some time and she already knows about you. They did look pretty goddamn familiar with each other in that cute little photo! Call one of your friends who is also friends with your boyfriend and have them friend request the slut. Then, have her send her a message saying how cute they look in that photo and then, very nonchalantly, ask her how long they have been seeing each other. Tell your friend to say that she is a good friend of your boyfriend and that she is so happy he met somebody. Then you'll get a straight answer out of the lying whore!

→ **OPTION #3**

Play your own game. Get a hot guy friend of yours and post a picture on Facebook of your own that seems to suggest a little more than friendship. If your man complains, attack him for being the pig that he is.

You and your friends having fun	You and your friends doing drugs
You and your dog	You getting a Pap smear
You doing something adventurous, like skydiving or mountain climbing	You getting arrested
You and your new tramp stamp	You and your new Brazilian wax
You in any photo in which you look deceptively thin	Your grandmother looking deceptively alive at her open-casket wake
Cancun	Drunk
Hedonism	Slutty

54. He is still friends with his supermodel ex-girlfriend

It's not that she is that much prettier than you. Well, okay, who's kidding who here—she is that much prettier than you. She is the kind of pretty that is almost sickening, her face so perfect it makes you want to smash it with an ugly stick. Just knowing that women like that exist is painful enough, let alone knowing that your ex was dating her before you. Add insult to injury by the fact that he still talks to her and you have a recipe for disaster. OMG—is that her *again* on the phone? AH!

→ OPTION #1

Confront her. Ask her why she's still hanging around. She should be out there finding a new man. The fact is she could probably have any man so tell this super hot bitch to get out of your man's life—for good!

→ OPTION #2

Make him choose. Her friendship or your love. Sure, he'll resent you forever, but what's a relationship without some deep resentment on both sides?

→ OPTION #3

Go all single white female on her. Copy the way she dresses, her hair, and get implants so, like her, you actually have breasts. Mimic her British accent, and fly to China for a surgery pioneered there to increase your height by a couple of inches, making you tall and graceful like her. Sure they have to break your leg bones a little bit, but no pain no gain, right? Oh, and you might want to stop eating and exercise constantly. You know, like the way she does?

→ OPTION #4

Disfigure her. This can be done in several ways, all of which are naturally illegal. A little gasoline and a match, a spiked baseball bat, or my personal favorite, sewing her butt closed and then feeding her chocolate for days until she explodes like a balloon.

→ OPTION #5

Stay strong. Look, he's dating you now—not her. Maybe they truly are just good friends and he wants nothing more than that. If you come across all jealous and shit this might drive a wedge in your relationship. Men love confident women so try to be okay with it.

OMG in Real Life

I live in Hollywood so every other girl I meet—including my new neighbor—seems to be a model. The day she moved in she was half naked, prancing up and down my block like it was a catwalk. I walked out of my apartment building and she came running up to me all excited and was like, "Hey I'm your new neighbor, so nice to meet you!" I smiled and said, "Welcome to the neighborhood." But what I wanted to do was run her over with my car. Okay, maybe a little nasty of me but she ruined my morning cupcake damn it!

—Courtney

In the Future...

Make sure you're the hottest girl he's ever dated.

55. He's a total drama queen

Guys. You can't live with them—and even the best vibrator can't fix a leak under the sink. Despite all odds, we have learned to live with these creatures and their many faults such as poor hygiene, bad table manners, and an almost pathological inability to put down a toilet seat after urinating. Those are the kind of annoying traits we as women are used to. But a whiny baby who wears his emotions on his sleeve? That is just not something we ladies can easily grapple with. What to do when your boyfriend is more emotional than you?

→ STEP #1

Check his genitals. Even if you have seen him many times naked, he still might have been a woman at one point before getting a sex change. Photograph his package and take it to the nearest doctor who specializes in sexual reassignment surgery for their opinion. Maybe there is a compelling biological imperative for your man to act like a little bitch.

→ STEP #2

Drink. Become a drunk in order to deal with all his emotional episodes and erratic, nagging behavior.

That's what most men turn to when their women drive them nuts.

→ STEP #3

Medicate him. Some men just can't deal with their PMS cycles so pump him full of Midol and call it a day.

→ STEP #4

Go down on him more. Sometimes men get really, really bitchy if you don't give them the oral pleasure that they need. However, make a note never to do Step #4 and Step #3 during the same seventy-two-hour period.

56. He's too broke to take you anywhere halfway decent

You just can't win. The last guy you dated was loaded but getting him out of the house was impossible. He was always tired from work, or at least that's what he said. But now you have the opposite problem: a fun-loving, adventurous guy who has champagne taste but a beer budget. He would love to wine and dine you. Unfortunately, his idea of wining and dining is a Taco Bell value meal washed down with a warm domestic beer. Yum!

→ **OPTION #1**

Get creative. Broke dudes can still have fun. Do a picnic on the beach instead of dining at a fancy restaurant overlooking the water. Throw more parties at home with friends instead of going out for happy hour. Check your local paper and websites for farmer's markets and other street fairs that are free to get into. Of course, make sure to fill up on Taco Bell before you get there. Oh, and don't forget to go shopping at fancy stores, wear the dress once, and take it back.

→ **OPTION #2**

Get tough. You know he has potential, which is what drew you to him to begin with. It is only a matter of time before his finger paintings sell for hundreds of thousands of dollars when he finally gets the international recognition he deserves. But until then, he might want to take a second job. You know, one that actually pays.

→ OPTION #3

Chill out. Who cares if he has no money—you can survive on love, right? Well that's what people say anyway. The fact is, if you really like this guy then this shit shouldn't matter. You just worry about your income. Maybe *you* can become super rich and he can be Mr. Mom one day.

Dating on a Budget

There are lots of things you guys can still do without a lot of money, such as:

- Sex
- Rent a movie
- Have him cook you dinner
- Sex
- Give each other massages
- Free concerts in the park
- Sex
- Hiking
- Going to the beach
- Sex

57. Your man would rather play video games than play with your boobs

The only thing more boring than staying home night after night is staying home night after night and not having sex. You feel like you constantly give him the opportunity but that he is just not interested in you sexually anymore. All he seems to care about are those damn video games, which he plays relentlessly. What to do when your man prefers his Xbox to *your* box?

→ OPTION #1

Smash the TV. Throw it out; it's no good for your brain anyhow. Books are better for the noggin, particularly sex books. And my books, of course.

→ OPTION #2

Spice it up. Buy some sexy lingerie from Victoria's Secret and prance around the house. If you still can't get to first base, then move on to Option #3.

→ OPTION #3

Take the lingerie off and walk around naked. If he still doesn't respond, dump his ass.

→ OPTION #4

Forget the lingerie, dress up like one of the characters from his favorite video games and do some role playing. Yeah, Lara Croft likes it nasty, big boy.

58. You got him an iPad for Christmas and he got you a gift certificate to Applebee's

You've been saving your money for over a month because the holidays were coming and you really wanted to get your guy something special. He kept talking about how much he wanted an iPad and all the cool things he would be able to do with it. Finally, you feel great because that's exactly what you got him. Sure, it cost you more than you wanted to spend but you can't put a price on a great gift. You wrapped it in gorgeous paper, got a thoughtful card, and couldn't wait to see his face when he opened it. When you exchange gifts, he ripped open his present and almost screamed when he saw his new toy. Score! Now it's your turn—he hands you your gift to open. Okay, it looks just like a card but you know what they say about good things coming in small packages. So you open it and there, before your eyes, is a $25 gift card to Applebee's. You almost giggle. Where's your real gift? OMG, that is the real gift? It's not the thought that counts. You spent all your hard earned money on this tool and you got a gift card to a crappy chain restaurant. Bullshit!

→ OPTION #1

Be a happy patriot, not an ungrateful, anti-American snot. Consider yourself lucky for getting a gift certificate to America's favorite restaurant. The sample platter? Are you kidding? It's the best, most interesting and varied dish in America, if not the world. There are two kinds of people in this country: those who like Applebee's and those who like Al Qaeda. What side are you on?

→ OPTION #2

Just stare at him. That's it, just like that. Maybe you are imagining this nightmare. Pinch yourself. If you are indeed awake, pinch *him* instead—hard.

→ OPTION #3

Use it. Take him out to Applebee's and dump his ass.

Jewelry	Fake jewelry
Clothes	Gym membership
Gift certificates for a massage	Handwritten IOU for a massage
Pretty lingerie	Box of condoms
Telling her you love her	Telling her you like her—a lot

→ OPTION #4

Be grateful. At least he got you something. Yes, it pales in comparison to your gift but giving really is better than receiving. Consider yourself lucky to even have a boyfriend at all. Some girls are always alone on the holidays, ya know, sitting around with their cats writing books like this one.

In the Future...

Tell your guy what you want. Trust me. Guys hate buying gifts but if you make it easy for him and tell him what you want, you'll both be happy.

59. He steals the covers every. frickin'. night.

Like a lot of quirks that are initially charming, this habit of his to steal the covers while he sleeps leaving you waking up cold and shivering has become pretty goddamn annoying. Why can't he just share the covers? What is he, against sharing? He's selfish, that's what it is. Downright selfish just like all men. Wait, breathe, relax. You could be overreacting. Consider these options instead. . . .

→ **OPTION #1**

Sleep with one eye open. Like the cowboys used to do. Catch that sucker in the act and let him have it!

→ **OPTION #2**

Buy another set of covers. Ever think of that, genius? Get two sets of covers. If he tries to steal yours too, strangle him in his sleep. Use his covers to wrap the body and then dump it in the river, drive back home, curl up, and sleep like a warm, happy baby.

→ OPTION #3

Become cold blooded. This is hard to do and requires a lot of surgery. Go to a veterinarian who specializes in reptiles and have him turn your warm-blooded mammalian biological system into that of a cold-blooded snake.

→ OPTION #4

Get a sleeping bag. He can't steal it if you're zipped up in it, right? Remember how much fun it was to get into your Care Bears sleeping bag, all warm and fuzzy? Go buy a new one and be nice and warm. It will make it kinda hard to have sex, but do you really want to have sex in a Care Bears sleeping bag? Perv.

Other Things You Never Want Your Guy to Steal
- Your heart
- Your car
- Your identity
- Your faith in humanity
- Your virginity

60. He wants your perky Bs upgraded to ridiculously huge DDs

Boobs. Tits. Ta-tas. Jugs. Cans. The list of euphemisms for the two pieces of concentrated fat that hang off our chest goes on and on. Clearly, men love breasts—the bigger the better. But the fact is you are happy with your average breasts and have no interest in turning yourself into a plastic Barbie doll, or worse, Heidi Montag. Then again, you want to make him happy. Whatever you do, consider it carefully. You're the one who has to lug those jugs around.

→ OPTION #1

Tell him he needs his own enhancement. Agree that sure, you will let some doctor cut you open with a knife and stuff your chest with sacks of silicone for his enjoyment if he gets a penile implant to satisfy yours. You like bigger boobs? Well, we like bigger you-know-whats. Dolly Parton meets Ron Jeremy. Now there's a sexy thought. . . .

→ OPTION #2

Leave him and keep your boobs. You are perfect just as you are, the way God intended, which in this case is flat as a board. If he doesn't love you as you are, then drop him like a bad habit.

→ OPTION #3

Keep your boobs and stay with him. Stand your ground. If you like the way you look then tell him that you won't change for anyone. If he loves you, he'll understand.

→ OPTION #4

Get new boobs and stay with him. Now that you think of it, it really would be nice to fill out a sweater and show some cleavage once in a while. Might make you feel more feminine. Oh, what the hell, why not?

→ OPTION #5

Get new boobs and leave him. Do as he suggests, and get your tits blown up to epic proportions. Once you get the bigger, better boobs, you might met a bigger, better guy.

Karma!

61. His jokes go over like a fart in church

Guys always tease us girls that we don't really think that "sense of humor" is the most important quality in a man. That's true. There's a reason the cliché is "tall, dark, and handsome," not "short, fat, and hysterical." Between Clive Owen and Seth Rogen we'll choose Clive any day of the week. That said, I bet Seth Rogen has more money. Either way, the point is that laughter is not always the way into a woman's heart. And you didn't fall in love with your guy for his sense of humor either, though he is pretty funny one on one. But when you get him to a party, you're not asking for a comedian—but does he really have to be that unbearably unfunny around people? Why is it that he feels the need to play the clown in public? Doesn't the fact that no one is laughing make any impression on him? OMG, not the one about the rabbit and the priest on a fishing boat again. Somebody stop him!

→ STEP #1

Confront him. Come right out and explain to your man that he might not be as funny as he thinks he is, and that he has plenty of other attributes to show off other than his humor. Like his biceps, for instance, or his extensive knowledge of ancient weapons of war.

→ STEP #2

Develop a secret code. Now that he is aware that he is not Mr. Funnyman, he is probably more embarrassed about his bad jokes than you are. Develop a code with him so that you can alert him in a social situation if he is having too many drinks, and therefore telling too many bad jokes. A lift of an eyebrow, a clearing of the throat, or a kick in the groin are all good ways to subtly let him know to shut his trap.

→ STEP #3

Make him take a comedy class. Even the most comically handicapped people can learn from a good stand-up comedy class. Whatever, he may not end up being the next Steve Martin, at least he'll learn that every good joke has one thing in common: a punchline!

Sense of Humor Goes a Long Way

Would you date these guys if they weren't so funny?

- Jack Black
- Dax Shepard
- Seth Rogen
- Russell Brand
- Jonah Hill

62. Cliché or not—that bastard *never* stops to ask for directions . . . EVER!

Men have a kind of primitive pride that expresses itself in odd ways—like their unwillingness to ask a stranger for directions even if they have no friggin' clue where they are or where they are going. With GPS, the problem of male stubbornness in this regard has been greatly relieved. But as we all know, even if you are lucky enough to have a navigation system in your car these modern marvels are by no means perfect. Sometimes you get lost. But your man is just too damn proud to ask for help. OMG, how the hell are you ever going to get to where you're going?

→ OPTION #1

Try blackmail. Like a total psycho, yell, "If you don't stop right now I will never have sex with you again!" Shoot him a look like you mean it and see how fast he'll hit the brakes. If he doesn't, then he either knows that you are a sex-crazed nymphomaniac who could only be bluffing or he isn't attracted to you anymore. Maybe he is getting lost on the way on purpose because he is delaying your inevitable sex advance tonight. OMG . . . he hates you!

→ OPTION #2

Emasculate him. Make fun of him for being lost and then tell him that "real men don't get lost." Of course, it is an obscenely stupid thing to say, but trust me it will break his heart. While he whimpers like a bitch, take charge of the wheel—and your night.

→ OPTION #3

Do nothing and get lost. Sit there quietly and watch as he drives you across three state lines into redneck country where serial killers and werewolves live. Act like you don't care as you watch him spiral out of control, trying to figure out what the hell to do. Eventually he will turn to you and ask for help, then you can refer to Option #1. You will help him this one time, but he owes you big now.

OMG Fact

He could benefit from a GPS system in the car *and* in the bedroom. 'Cause we all know he doesn't ask for directions in there either.

In the Future...

Insist on driving. If he lets you, he may not be a real man, but at least you won't end up circling the same block over and over and over again until the sun comes up.

>> 63. His place is condemnable and you have five roommates

God it's gross. How can guys live this way? The bathroom, the kitchen, the bedroom, it all looks the same—dirty. You can't even tell which room is which. You love seeing him but you can't stand coming back to his rat hole. If it wasn't for your five friggin' roommates you would bring him to your place, which is cleaner than his despite the crowd.

→ **OPTION #1**

Move in with him. Okay, he is a pig but you love him, right? Not to mention the five roommate thing is a bit annoying. Invade his space (if he'll have you) and whip his filthy ass into shape. Make him do daily chores, including shining your heels. Time to show him who's boss.

→ **OPTION #2**

Get him a maid. Buy him a maid to clean up after him. You should have some extra money if you live with five roommates. Then again, if you did have extra money you wouldn't live with five roommates. Damn. Move on to Option #3.

→ **OPTION #3**

Relocate together. You leave your sorority house and have him live with you. Start fresh and clean for that matter.

64. His breath smells like ass

Bad breath can be the result of various things: Rotten teeth, halitosis, or, more typically, punishment for being a real jerk in a previous life. He's so cute, your man. So charming. So sexy. And OMG he has the nicest lips! Too bad that the minute he opens them the whole room smells like shit. How important is kissing anyway? Really important, damn it!

→ OPTION #1

Altoids. Preferably the peppermint, which is stronger than the spearmint or the wintergreen kind.

→ OPTION #2

Seek help. Many times bad breath is a symptom caused by an underlying medical or dental condition. Take your guy to the doctor and hopefully he can get to the bottom of the dumpster mouth problem.

→ OPTION #3

Seek God. When Altoids, dental work, and tongue removal fail, time to elicit the help of our Lord Jesus Christ. Not only is he the Son of God, he was known for having excellent breath.

→ OPTION #4

Fight fire with fire, or in this case shit. Eat lots of garlic, onions, and anything else that makes your breath stink. When he comments on your breath, inform him that's what it's like kissing him. Trust me, after that he will immediately try to find a solution on his own.

65. Your boyfriend is that guy

When you first met him, the fact that he seemed like the kind of guy that could protect you appealed to you. You like a man to be a man, tough, confident, and protective. So when he tells a guy at the bar who's hitting on you to "take a hike," you can't help but find it attractive. But the more you go out with him you start to notice a trend. Your guy is *always* looking for a fight. Now you're starting to think it would be nice to grab some sushi without your boyfriend threatening to slice the waiter into sashimi.

→ **OPTION #1**

Talk to him. Maybe he'll try and calm down. Then again, if he could work things out by talking he probably wouldn't resort to punching a guy's face in every time.

→ **OPTION #2**

Get him anger management. Looks like he might need counseling. Better you sign him up to take some anger management classes than wait until it's court ordered.

→ **OPTION #3**

Get turned on. Come on, you know you like it when your man defends your honor and his. Nothing is sexier than a man you love bashing a stranger's head. Is it your fault that you get hot when you see your man's T-shirt soaked in another man's blood?

→ OPTION #4

Run, fast! This is a giant red flag. It's only a matter of time before this testosterone head brings the fight home. Why risk it? Dump his ass and find a lovable nerd. They're very trendy right now—and often rich, too!

Is Your Boyfriend Too Tough?

There is such a thing as being too tough, even for a guy:

- Instead of using an ashtray to put out his cigarette, he uses his left eyeball.
- When you accidentally spilled boiling water on his back while boiling potatoes, he laughed and threw some on you too, thinking it was a game.
- When you're going down town, he likes it when you bite.

In the Future...

Date a pretty boy. They tend not to get into fights as much for the fear that someone will hit their face.

66. You say "I love you," he says "thanks"

Saying "I love you" is a serious step in a relationship, and often scares men out of their wits. Men are far more likely to say three word phrases such as "Please touch it," or "I am clean" or "Split the check?" long before and with much more ease than those three dreaded words. But you have been dating this guy for a few months now, and it's obvious that you both have strong feelings for one another. So when you turn to him and say, "I love you" for the first time and he responds with "Um, thanks" you can't help but be thrown and hurt. "Thanks!" Really? OMG?

→ **OPTION #1**

Make him love you. That's right; force him to love you just like you plan to force him to change. Of course, this is a futile venture, but you might as well try. After all, you wouldn't be the first girl to waste years of her life trying to force a man to feel something he doesn't.

→ **OPTION #2**

Ask him. Maybe he is the strong and silent type. Guys have a harder time showing emotions, so he might be deeply in love with you but just too shy to say it. Remember, men show their affection in funny ways like mowing the lawn or getting a vasectomy reversal. Put him in the hot seat and find out just how he truly feels.

→ OPTION #3

Cry. Alone, in the bathroom, sob your eyes out. Then instead of taking it out on him or breaking up with him and searching for a man, who actually does love you, turn that sadness inward and embark on a ruthless journey of self-punishment.

→ OPTION #4

Dump him. Drown yourself temporarily in chocolate and ice cream and then get back out there and find your soul mate.

Test Your Love IQ

1. Love is:
   A. Blind
   B. All you need
   C. Never having to say you're sorry
   D. A crock of shit

2. To love is to:
   A. Suffer
   B. Experience the height of human irrationality
   C. Worry about losing half your shit when it eventually dies out
   D. Horniness turned weird
   E. All of the above

3. The strongest kind of love is love between:
   A. A man and a woman
   B. Two men
   C. Two women
   D. Father and son
   E. Mother and son
   F. Father and daughter
   G. Mother and daughter
   H. Jennifer Aniston and whomever she is dating at the time

Answer Key: 1: A; 2: D; 3: H, obvi.

67. You've been dating for years and motherf#@*er still hasn't proposed

After the first few months of dating you started seeing each other exclusively. After the first year of dating you moved in together. After the second year together your families celebrated the holidays together. Yep. Things were progressing nicely, just as they should. Fast forward three more years and nothing has changed. Still no ring? What's the deal? He loves me, I love him. When will it happen?! As each year goes by, more and more of your friends are getting married but not you! OMG is he ever going to propose?

→ OPTION #1

Pull a Marisa Tomei in *My Cousin Vinny*. Make a gigantic scene, screaming and stomping the floor. It worked in the movie, and your man is much more of a pussy than Joe Pesci.

→ OPTION #2

Stay unmarried. There are plenty of couples that never got married that live happy and fulfilling lives together: Goldie Hawn and Kurt Russell, Gene Simmons and Shannon Tweed, Siegfried and Roy, just to name a few.

→ OPTION #3

Make subtle hints. Let him know that you think it is time to move the relationship forward by dropping subtle hints. Point out old married couples and "how happy they look." Mention every time one of your friends is getting married. Push him down on his knees and shout, "Where's my ring, asshole?" Stuff like that.

→ OPTION #4

Common law. In some jurisdictions, if a couple has been living together and held themselves out to the world as husband and wife for a significant period of time it can be known as a common law marriage. This means you have a lot of the same rights as a married couple just none of the benefits, like a wedding, or a ring, or the gifts. Screw this, go back to Option #1.

→ OPTION #5

Ask him. Hey, it's the twenty-first century. If you know he loves you and you love him, then drop to one knee and pop the question. Hey, Monica did it to Chandler on *Friends*. Sure, that's just a sitcom but it does happen. Odds are if you're down on one knee he won't say no—to anything.

Best Ways to Get Engaged

- On vacation
- On top of the Empire State Building
- In a hot air balloon

Worst Ways

- After you tell him you're pregnant
- When he's in prison
- As an ultimatum

68. You make way more money than him

First of all, pat yourself on the back, girl, for making it in a man's world. But there is a price to pay for all this success and power. A lot of men find success threatening—and your man is no different. At first he acted like he didn't care that you made way more than him, but now you know that's not true. He hates it and it's starting to really affect your relationship.

→ OPTION #1

Pay him to stop being a baby. Tell him that you'll give him a bigger allowance if he shuts up and just deals with the fact that you are more successful. With this second job, he'll make more and you'll bring in less—should even things out.

→ OPTION #2

Make him feel like a man in other ways. If he is not feeling like a man because you are the main bread-winner, then tell him he has a big penis—even if it's not true. Also make sure to act really impressed when he hangs a picture on the wall, plunges a toilet, grills a hamburger, or does any other stupid thing guys believe only they can do well.

→ OPTION #3

Encourage him to be more ambitious. If he hates his job then help him "find himself." Or just buy him a new sporty car. That should shut him up for a while.

→ OPTION #4

Do nothing. If he can't handle the fact that you are more successful than him, so be it. Don't apologize for your success. Celebrate it and if he can't get over it, then let him leave. Then find yourself a more successful man or one who isn't threatened by you. Snap!

These Men Couldn't Handle Their Women Bringing Home the Bacon

- Jesse James cheated on Sandra Bullock
- Guy Ritchie left Madonna
- Courtney Cox and David Arquette split
- Ryan Phillippe cheated on Reese Whitherspoon

These Couples Can Handle It

- Julia Roberts and Daniel Moder
- Oprah and Stedman
- Sarah Jessica Parker and Matthew Broderick

Though rumor is he cheated, too.

69. He thinks you're his mommy

When you first started dating him, you liked taking care of him to a point but now it's gotten a little out of control. He expects you to wash his clothes, make him dinner, and keep track of all his important papers and dates. He wants you to bring him soup when he is sick, ice cream when he has a tooth-ache, and tuck him in when he is sleepy. It's like living with an infant—one grown ass infant.

→ OPTION #1

Punish him. If you are going to get to play mommy, then that should mean you get to be in charge, too. Give him a list of chores to do every day like making a bubble bath for you and giving you a foot massage for a few hours.

→ OPTION #2

Get another man. Get rid of this zero and get with a hero. Then realize that all men are whiny babies and date chicks instead.

→ OPTION #3

Adopt him. If he is going to act like your son, then officially make him your son by adopting him. Cite him as a dependant now and save money at tax time.

→ OPTION #4

Retrain him. Look, this behavior was learned. So be his second mommy and teach him how to take care of himself as well as you. Men are very moldable; just reward his good behavior with treats.

Is Your Man Too Infantile?

- When he has to go number two, he refers to it as "number two"
- When he pees, he prefers to wear pants
- When he sucks your nipples, he complains that "nothing happens"
- He asks "why?" to everything over and over again
- He eats like Mommy's little piggie

Benefits to Dating a Mama's Boy

- He doesn't hate all women
- He'll let you dress him
- You can guilt him into almost anything

70. He wants a long-distance relationship

Your boyfriend has just been offered his dream job. Too bad that job is in another state. He's leaving but he doesn't want to break up. He wants to try the long-distance thing. Ah, the long-distance relationship. It's a fable, an urban legend, a myth. There have been rumors that it has worked before but there is no historical record proving it. While absence makes the heart grow fonder initially, eventually, it makes the heart stop giving a shit.

→ **OPTION #1**

Move with him. Come to the airport with him and then at the last minute run after the plane and say that you want to go with him, just like in the movies. Then go buy a ticket for a later date since that flight is already full. Change your mind again while waiting for your flight and head home. To inform him that you are not coming anymore, just post something on your Facebook page.

→ **OPTION #2**

Have phone sex. Or even better, cyber sex through Skype. It may not be as good as the real thing, but at least you can't get herpes.

→ **OPTION #3**

Make him get a penile extension, preferably one that can cross four states, a mountain range, and three rivers.

→ OPTION #4

Enjoy it. Seriously, this could be the best thing. A part-time boyfriend. You visit him, he'll visit you, and before he can start to annoy you the visit's over. This could be exactly what you need. Until you find another hottie in your city, then dump his long-distance ass!

→ OPTION #5

Let the relationship die out slowly. Try your best to see him and do your best to talk to him. You will both make the effort, but inevitably the relationship will fail and you'll fall in love with a new asshole.

→ OPTION #6

Get pregnant fast. That way he'll have to be in your life forever. Or at least the next eighteen years.

In the Future...

Date a guy with no aspirations of achieving anything great so he'll never leave you or leave town.

71. After a year of dating he stills refers to you as his "good friend"

It's been a year. Twelve solid months of dates, sleepovers, weekend getaways—the works. You are in this great relationship with a terrific guy so why is it whenever he introduces you to people he still refers to you as his "good friend"? Did the definition of "good friend" change? When you think of a good friend you think of someone you grab coffee with, maybe lunch. Someone you catch an afternoon movie with or help move into a new apartment. That's a good friend. When did "good friend" also mean someone who you exchange bodily fluids with?

→ **OPTION #1**

Be honest. Tell him how you feel. He might not even be aware he's doing it. Explain to him that it's been a year and if he really doesn't consider you his "girlfriend" then maybe you should move on to another "good friend."

→ **OPTION #2**

Correct him. The next time he says, "This is my good friend, Taylor," you add, "Who makes him breakfast in the morning after he has sex with me, nice to meet you." That might be shocking but I bet that will be the last time he introduces you like that.

→ OPTION #3

Embrace it. Okay, so you're his "good friend"—be proud. Get T-shirts made up that say "I'm Charlie's Good Friend." Sign your name to everything, "Good friend of Charlie's." The more you own it, the more you will learn to like it. I now pronounce you good friends!

→ OPTION #4

Give him a new title. The next time you introduce him, say, "This is Charlie, the guy I love to have sex with after a night of drinking." Two can play at this game, sucka!

This is my bud.	This is the guy who I get wasted with and will cover my ass if I cheat on my girlfriend.
She's just someone I met once.	We hooked up and I blew her off.
She's a bitch.	I hit on her and she shot me down.
She's a good girl.	I haven't slept with her yet, but I am trying to.
I love you.	I don't know if I love you but I have a feeling I have to say it sooner or later or you'll leave me.

chapter 5

BFFs That Make You Say "WTH?!"

OMG!

72. Your friends hate him

They never say it directly but it's obvious that your friends aren't his biggest fans. When you mention he's coming out with you guys, they sometimes don't show up. When they do see him, they force a smile and try to hide their dislike, but never successfully. Maybe they are seeing something you're not, or maybe they are just jealous. OMG, what to do?!

→ **OPTION #1**

Dump him. Your friends know you better than you know yourself. Maybe you aren't seeing something they are. Make them explain to you what they don't like about him.

→ **OPTION #2**

Tell your friends to shove it. Hey, if he's the man you love, then he's the man you love. As friends, they should accept that and do their best to support you in whatever decisions you make. Maybe they're just jealous.

→ **OPTION #3**

Let them sleep with him. Maybe it is jealousy after all. If this is the case, then let your friends get some of your man's good lovin' so they won't be so hard up anymore.

→ **OPTION #4**

Have your boyfriend set them up. If you don't want your boyfriend to have sex with your friends, have him find them their own boyfriends to screw. That will show them that he cares about not only your happiness but theirs. If they still hate him, go to Option #2.

My best friend was dating this total asshole. Everyone including her family hated this guy, but for some reason she thought he was amazing. So I started a rumor that I saw him kissing another girl. She confronted him and he denied it, but that was enough to plant a seed of doubt in her mind. They broke up and we were all thrilled. About 4 years later I finally came clean and she was pissed. I mean really mad—so mad that she ended our friendship as well. My point is, sometimes you just need to let your friends do their thing and deal with their own choices—even when you want to frickin' kill them.

—Amy

73. His friends hate you

No matter how nice you are to his pals they just don't seem to like you. They don't say it outright, but you know it's the case. You have women's intuition, you just know it. Sure they smile and they say hello and they show all the outward signs of politeness, but deep down they want you out of the picture. They are jealous of you, and miss the good ol' times when their buddy was a raging alcoholic, women-chasing moron just like they are.

And then your suspicions are confirmed when you overhear them talking shit at a party about your boyfriend getting tied down by a chick with cankles. Bastards!

→ **OPTION #1**

Kill them with kindness. Be so nice it makes them sick. Cook for them, offer them a beer in an ice cold mug whenever they are over, giggle and bat your eyes at everything they say. Basically, be so annoyingly nice and charming that they cannot help but start to dig you.

→ **OPTION #2**

Screw them . . . metaphorically. Hey, they don't like you, that's their problem. They are going to have to get used to you either way because this chick ain't going nowhere. Got that, pal?

→ OPTION #3

Screw them . . . literally. Listen, you know they are just mad because they want to tap that ass. So give it to them and be done with it. They may not respect you, but they'll sure as hell like you a lot more!

→ OPTION #4

Get them screwed . . . literally. Hook them up with your hot girl-friends. They'll be happy, your girlfriends will be happy, and your boyfriend will be happy. You're a freakin hero!

OMG Quick Tips for Getting His Friends to Warm Up

Remember things about them: Like their birthdays, or when his buddy Joe shit himself in church

Let them teach you something: Like how to grill the perfect steak or pole dance

When you go somewhere with your boyfriend, ask his friends if they want to come: Like to Bed Bath & Beyond, or just to bed

If you have an interest in some-thing, tell them about it: Like scrapbooking, *Gossip Girl*, and noncommittal sex

NOTE: If one of your boyfriend's friends is a girl, get rid of her, that can't ever be good.

>>> 74. His best friend hits on you

Out of all your man's friends, his best friend Joe is your absolute favorite. He is a great friend, and a great guy all around. He's always polite and charming, though he is a bit of a flirt. He compliments what you wear and calls you "sweetheart," but it's all in good fun. That is, until one night he gets drunk at your man's birthday party and grabs you in the hall—his hands and his tongue all over you. OMG!

→ **OPTION #1**

Screw him. Come on, you know you want to.

→ **OPTION #2**

Screw him—but in a metaphorical way—by telling your man. When your man bashes his face in he'll feel more screwed than ever.

→ **OPTION #3**

Blackmail him. You might as well turn a bad situation into a better one. Well, for you anyway. Push the creep off of you and then threaten to tell your man unless he pays up. Then, use the money to take your boyfriend out and buy things that his friend always wanted to get, digging the knife in even deeper.

→ OPTION #4

Let yourself go. Stop waxing, eat your feelings, and stop bathing. You will never have to worry about someone hitting on you again. Including your boyfriend.

→ OPTION #5

Um, threesome, hello? Especially if he's hot.

In the Future...

Date a guy with no friends. Not only does this solve the problem but your man will want to spend all his time with you—'cause he has no friends!

Leans in for a kiss	Spit in his mouth
Squeezes your ass	Squeeze his throat, until he blacks out
Sends you a love letter	Send him a restraining order

75. You have the hots for your boyfriend's roommate

At first you barely even looked at him—he wasn't your type anyway. Too much of a pretty boy, you would say. You like them rougher, more manly—like your burly boyfriend. But the more you spend time with your man when his roommate is around the more you start to experience these strange feelings. His smile, his sparkling blue eyes, and his body—lean and way more cut and muscular than you would think. And he's so smart, well read, and interesting. What charm, like an old movie star. Uh oh. You have a wild crush on your boyfriend's roommate. OMG!

→ **OPTION #1**

Stay calm. Remember, no one can know your innermost thoughts. Just because when you look at him you get chills, doesn't mean that he (or your man) will put 2 and 2 together. That said, you might want to put your tongue back in your mouth . . . he's looking!

→ **OPTION #2**

Confess. If you really think you are into this guy, come right out and tell him how you feel. Just to be polite, you might wait until your boyfriend leaves the room. You know, it's a respect thing.

→ **OPTION #3**

Threesome? Just kidding. Well . . .

→ OPTION #4

Have an affair. If you like your man but you just can't control yourself, sleep with the roommate and see if he is any good. You might not be as compatible as you imagined. Be careful though, there is at least a .0001% chance that he will turn you down and tell your man.

→ OPTION #5

End it. The relationship that is. This can only lead to trouble. Either you will end up cheating on your man, or you'll just be miserable every time you see his roommate. Then after some time apart see if you still have feelings for his roommate, if so . . . pounce!

In the Future...

Don't date a guy with a roommate, or friends or brothers.

What NOT to Do

- Drink. A lot. Around him. Really, really bad idea
- Hang out there when your boyfriend's not home
- Lie naked in his bed waiting for him.
- Sniff his underwear

OMG in Real Life

At first I hated my boyfriend's best friend. I would tell my boyfriend that I didn't want him hanging out with this guy 'cause he was an asshole. He was sarcastic and rude and always knew how to push my buttons. Then one day it hit me: *I don't hate him—I really like him.* I really wanted him. One night after many drinks we hooked up. I felt so bad that I told my boyfriend. We broke up and I started to date his best friend. Turns out he was an asshole after all; he ended up cheating on me. That's karma I guess.

—Christine

76. Your friends are convinced he's gay

Okay, so from the outside you can see how they might think that. Your man does like musical theatre, *Project Runway*, and it was him that convinced you to take ballroom dancing classes, not the other way around. But he's just metrosexual, right? I mean, you guys have sex. True, not very often and it's usually you that instigates it. And come to think of it he also curiously never wants to go down on you. And why does he always need to watch porn before sex—and never lesbian porn? OMG . . . are they right? Is he really gay? Time to find out.

→ STEP #1

Test his gayness. Tell him that Cher, Lady Gaga, and Madonna all just died in the same plane crash. If he sobs, screams, and threatens to take his own life because obviously this must be a godless universe for something so tragic to happen, then you have your answer.

→ STEP #2

Set him up. Pay a hot gay guy to come on to him someplace and see how he reacts. If he starts making out with him, there's your answer.

→ STEP #3

Accept it, and live happily ever after. If it turns out that he is gay, confront him about it and make him face the music. Then, live happily ever after like Will and Grace. Share your dreams, your secrets, and the occasional blow job story.

→ STEP #4

Stop the talk. Tell your friends to mind their business and worry about their own love life. Truth is they're probably jealous of your boyfriend. He's pretty and sensitive and he's probably a better girlfriend to you than your actual girlfriends.

Signs Your Guy Might Be Gay

He wears vintage Streisand concert T-shirts

He's a self-proclaimed "Gleek"

A girl walks by wearing a low cut top with her boobs hanging out and he says, "*Loves* the shirt"

He has more highlights in his hair than you

You catch him banging another dude

77. His friends are always over

Listen, it's not that you don't like his friends; it's just that you like them in small doses. But lately, these friends are over more and more and are staying longer and longer. What is this, a frat house? What happened to movie night with you and your man? Now it feels more like a cramped theater than it does an intimate night with the man you love. And OMG do they make a mess! And they always leave the friggin' lights on. Who are they working for, the electric company? Ahh!

→ **OPTION #1**

Confront your man—and his friends. You could just tell your man to limit how often his friends come over but maybe it's better to just let everyone hear your feelings directly from you. Tell them that while you like their company, every time you come home from work you take a deep breath before opening the door, and pray to God that they are not here. That'll send the message.

→ **OPTION #2**

Make an appointment. Set up a system in which your man's friends have to make an appointment before coming over. It's their fault for abusing the home. And now they have to deal with the consequences. Penalty of showing up unannounced? Death by hanging sounds reasonable.

→ OPTION #3

Charge rent. If you can't stop these assholes from hanging around your living room then you might as well make a buck or two off of them. Charge them rent and become the biggest bitch of a landlord you can be. Hopefully they'll start looking for another place.

→ OPTION #4

Fight fire with fire. He wants his friends over, fine; you like to walk around the house naked. It's your new thing, little or no clothes when you're in the privacy of your own home. If your boyfriend doesn't like that you're naked in front of his friends, he will make sure they don't come over ever, and you'll probably get a lot more sex now. Everyone's a winner.

The Right Way to Get His Friends to Leave

- You: Can you tell your friends to leave?
- Him: Why?
- You: 'Cause I want to have crazy sex with you right now.
- Him: Done.

The Wrong Way to Get His Friends to Leave

- You: Can you tell your friends to leave?
- Him: Why?
- You: 'Cause I want to cuddle up with you on the couch and watch a Lifetime movie.

In the Future...

Just always hang at your place.

78. He always tweets his friends after you have a fight

Technology can be a wonderful thing. It can bring people together, bridge the gap between cultural and geographical boundaries, and allow you to post an unlimited amount of pictures of your drunk ass at a club for the whole world to see. But technology, like other generally good things such as a dirty martini or the welfare system, can be abused. What happens when our private lives are no longer private? What happens when we feel obligated to share every detail of our lives with the rest of the world? What happens when your boyfriend tweets his pals—and yours—every time you guys have a fight? You follow these steps—that's what happens!

→ STEP #1

Fight tweet with tweet. Get on Twitter yourself and tweet something embarrassing about him (but not too embarrassing). For example, tell the funny story when you first saw him wearing a shower cap, rather than the fact that he found out he was adopted when he was 18.

In the Future…

If you sense you're about to have a fight, grab his phone and hide it so he can't tweet. If he's at home with his computer, smash the computer. Tweet that, asshole!

→ STEP #2

Answer his frantic call. He will most likely be calling you to yell at you about your tweet, so answer the phone and explain to him that it was his fault. Now comes the ultimatum: if he continues to share every detail of your relationship via Twitter then you will continue to tweet one embarrassing thing about him per day. Tell him that your plan for the third tweet is to tell everyone about the time he asked if he could wear your thong to work.

→ STEP #3

Add more to the ultimatum. Hey, this ultimatum thing really works! Might as well use it to your advantage. Make him clean the kitchen and give you massages for a month—that'll show him who's boss!

79. Your guy always wants to go on a group date

The annoying thing is that he was the one who never wanted to go out. Like a lot of guys, the minute you guys get serious he loses all personality and all desire to do anything with anyone. All he wanted to do was stay home or go out and watch a movie. You were always the one who wanted to meet friends and to hang out with friends and with other couples. Now, not only has the pendulum swung the other way but he insists that other people come whenever you do anything together. What is he now, Mr. Social? Well, it seems that way. You knew it was out of hand when he suggested he invite his buddies from work to your anniversary dinner. OMG is he nuts?

→ OPTION #1

Confront/guilt him. Step up to him and just ask him what the hell his problem is. Tell him your feelings, that you just don't appreciate the fact that he never wants to see you alone. What, are you not good enough for him? Make him answer for himself, damn it!

→ OPTION #2

Say nothing, but act weird. That's it, a very typically female approach. Say nothing and just be upset. Hold it in and try to punish him in other ways, like withholding sex. That will bring it to his attention that you are upset about a particular issue. He won't know what but he'll try real hard to fix it.

→ OPTION #3

Become a swinger. Perhaps he secretly desires to be a swinger. Maybe that's why he always wants to go out with other couples? Ask him if he is a pervert and then decide whether or not you are also a pervert if he answers in the affirmative. Hey, this could be a whole new exciting lifestyle waiting for you both!

→ OPTION #4

Dump him. Take your (and his) shit and leave town. You should be more than enough excitement for him and, if not, he doesn't deserve you!

→ OPTION #5

Sabotage his plans. Let him invite some other couples, then before the date, call them and cancel. Then you guys go out and when no one shows, *voila*! It's just you two. ↑

Sneaky but effective.

80. He's trying to steal your BFF

You were more than happy that you finally found a guy that likes your friends as much as you do—and they like him. He doesn't just insist on hanging out with his bar buddies like some of the other dudes you dated in the past. That said, he is getting a bit too close with your friends. Not close in the sense that he's having sex with a couple of them (that was your ex!), but close in the sense that he is becoming more of their BFF than you are! He even calls them for advice on how to deal with the problems in your relationship! OMG what is going on?

→ **OPTION #1**

Confront your friends. Tell them that while you love them and that you are pleased that they have, for the first time in memory, taken an interest in your boyfriend, enough is enough. Whose friend are they, exactly? Time to choose sides— him or me. It's decision time, bitches!

→ **OPTION #2**

Talk to him. Tell him that it is not his place to be speaking about your private life with your friends. Lay down the law and let him know that that kind of behavior is a really "no-no" in relationships. A deal breaker.

→ OPTION #3:

Make his friends your friends. Not that guys give a shit or are interested in anything that does not directly deal with them, but call his friends anyway and start getting their opinion on matters of the heart. They may fall asleep, but it's worth a shot.

Things Guys Ask For

- The remote
- Food
- Oral sex

Things Guys Never Ask For

- To meet your parents
- Directions
- Your opinion

81. He really, really wants to have a threesome with your best friend

Two women at the same time. It's every red-blooded man's ultimate fantasy. That's why guys are always doing everything they can to get girls to make out with each other at a party. They go nuts for it. So it's no surprise when your man inevitably brings it up. Typically you would say no as you have in the past, but this time you really, really like this guy and you want to make him happy. You don't want to lose him and you don't want to be a prude.

→ OPTION #1

Just say no. When conservative Nancy Reagan told a generation of teenagers to "Just Say No," she wasn't just talking about doing drugs, she was also talking about diddling your roommate while your man watches.

→ OPTION #2

Just say yes—to alcohol. Lots of it. Now you are ready to do just about anything you normally wouldn't do and you'll regret the next morning—just like you did in college.

→ OPTION #3

Tell him that you will have a threesome with your girlfriend if you could also have a three-some with another man. Fair is fair, right? There is only one problem with this option. He might say yes. OMG, now you are really in for it!

→ OPTION #4

Throw it in his face. He likes threesomes so bad, no problem. Go out and pick two random guys to have sex with. Tape it and give it to him on his birthday. That'll teach him, asshole!

82. You guys made a sex tape, and he showed it to his friends

Sex is a private and intimate experience. So the idea of taping yourself having sex was a little off-putting. But you want to make your man happy and you wanted to spice things up, so when he wanted to make a little porno for your own private usage, you agreed. Turns out it was actually kind of fun. You liked watching it with your man. But when you sit down at the computer and see his e-mail open you can't help but notice the subject line of the first e-mail all in caps: NICE SEX TAPE, BRO!

OMG. OMG. OMG. No, it can't be. You click the e-mail and it becomes painfully obvious that the e-mail is from his best friend Dave, and he is referring to your sex tape. Shit!

→ OPTION #1

Go. Ape. Shit. You know you are going to anyway. Trash his car, apartment, every DVD in his collection. If he thought he was screwed during the video, wait until he gets home—then he'll be really screwed! Then send a copy of the video to his parents and boss (only if you don't mind them seeing your hoo-ha); then the shit will really hit the fan. Karma's a bitch, baby; time for you to be one too!

→ OPTION #2

Get revenge. You are embarrassed, so embarrass him. Go swimming in a really, really, cool pool and then surreptitiously film him while he changes after some serious "shrinkage." Post it on YouTube and let the embarrassment begin!

→ OPTION #3

Cry. That's it, let it out, girl. You need a good cry. Now blow your nose, wipe away those tears, and go to Option #1—kick his fuckin' ass!

→ OPTION #4

Thank him for making you a star. Paris Hilton, Pamela Anderson, Kim Kardashian—all of these women have one thing in common. No, not herpes—but close. What they have in common is that each one of these celebrities either became famous or became more famous because a private video of them having sex became public domain. Forget about finishing that marketing master's, you are now going to be a famous whore. Dreams really do come true!

> I don't care about that tape, it just reminds the world of what they can't have.
> Paris Hilton

chapter 6

All in the Family

OMG!

83. He takes you to meet his parents on the second date

He was so creative the first time you guys met. Bungee jumping! Who would have thought of such an exciting and untraditional first date? You were so interested to see what he has in mind for your second date. A helicopter ride? Hang gliding? A bullfight? But while you were certainly surprised by his choice of venue, you weren't exactly ecstatic. His parents' house for dinner on a second date? Can someone say OMG?!

→ **STEP #1**

Breathe. Everything is going to be alright. Strange and awkward sure, but in the end all will be fine.

→ **STEP #2**

Smile. (But don't forget to keep breathing!)

→ **STEP #3**

Drink. A glass of wine should do. What? They're Mormons!? You didn't know that!

→ **STEP #4**

Eat. Well, at least you'll get a free meal out of it, which is better than half the dates you go on where the cheapskate wants to go Dutch. Smile, chat, eat up, and fill your belly until you are about to explode.

→ STEP #5

Emergency! Okay, now that you are full it's time for you to receive an emergency text. "OMG you won't believe what just happened," you say. A friend's car broke down, you left the stove on, your pug just committed suicide—say whatever it takes and get the hell out of Dodge.

→ STEP #6

Change your name and number. You never want to hear from that weirdo ever again. OR . . .

→ STEP #7

Embrace it. Hey, you might have just found the one guy who wants to be in a committed relationship immediately. This could be a good thing. If his family seems cool, go with it. The way things are going you'll be engaged in about a week. Congrats!

84. His father likes you— a little too much

At first you thought it was cute, just an charming older man being an charming older man. An occasional wink, a "sweetie" or two, a compliment on how beautiful you look. But now it seems whenever you see him he hangs on a little too long when you hug, he goes for the lips when you kiss goodbye, and he looks at you from across the dining room table like you're dessert. Yuck!

→ OPTION #1

Tell your man. Come right out and express your feelings about his perverted father. He might shrug his shoulders and laugh it off, or he might take a rifle and shoot his father between his eyes. Whatever he does it will be his decision. You've said your piece.

→ OPTION #2

Keep your mouth shut. If you don't see the old perv that often, just deal with it. It might not be worth causing major family drama. So your man's dad wants to play hide the salami with you? Big deal. If you were him, wouldn't you want to?

→ OPTION #3

Beat him at his own game. Start flirting back with his dad but at inappropriate places, like his office. Start sending e-mails and calling him. If he doesn't want his wife—or son for that matter—to find out he'll put an end to it pronto. Then you're off the hook, unless of course he takes the bait, then you are screwed—literally.

In the Future...

Look for a guy whose dad is gay. Problem solved.

OMG Rant

What's up with the phrase "Who's your daddy?" Who started that? What guy thought it was a good idea to bring up a girl's father during sex? More important, what girl was like, "Hey, ya know what would be super hot? If while we were having sex, you repeatedly asked me who my father was." I want to find that girl and punch her in the face, then flip the switch. The next time I have sex with a guy I'm gonna shout out, "Who's your mommy?" That should scare them enough never to ask that question again.

>> 85. You and his mother hate each other's guts

The two most important women in a man's life are his sweetheart and his mother. Even his secretary (who later becomes his new sweetheart) doesn't compare. It is critical for your man's mother to like you, as mothers wield a lot of influence and power—especially over men. There's a reason it's called "mama's boy" and "daddy's girl," and not vice-versa. Too bad his mother hates your guts and you can't stand her either. Uh oh.

→ **OPTION #1**

Tell your boyfriend. On second thought, don't be a moron and go directly to Option #2.

→ **OPTION #2**

Confront her. If you are sick of all the nasty glances and subtle hateful exchanges then just go to her and be direct. Tell her that you feel the same way about her as she feels about you, but for the sake of her son you need to get along.

→ **OPTION #3**

Take an acting class. If you can't seem to be able to contain your contempt for this old bag of bones then you might want to take some acting technique courses to help you learn the art of acting (lying).

86. He still lives at home and he has no intention of leaving

In many cultures around the world it is typical for a son or a daughter to live with their parents until they get married—even during college. So if he was from another country that would be understandable, but he's not. Yet he is 30 years old and still lives at home with mommy and daddy. OMG, move out already!

→ **OPTION #1**

Make him watch *Failure to Launch*. In this incredibly moving film, the always dreamy and always stupid Matthew McConaughey plays a man who just can't seem to leave the nest. Until, of course, he finds the love of a great woman. Maybe he will realize that, despite having far less abdominal definition, he and the protagonist have a lot in common. He might just get his act together—and get a six-pack in the process.

→ **OPTION #2**

Get help from his parents. Chances are that even if they don't say it to him mom and dad probably want their thirty-year-old son to get his own life and get the hell out of theirs—or at least their living room. The golden years are golden for a reason—you finally got rid of everyone else who drove you nuts. Elicit help from his folks—you might be surprised just how on board they are.

→ OPTION #3

Move in with them. Hey, if you can't beat 'em, join 'em. Maybe it isn't so bad after all? Just because you can't stand your parents doesn't mean that you won't love living with his. Free rent, free food, and a free old lady to clean shit up. Maybe your man isn't so crazy after all.

→ OPTION #4

Have him move in with you. Hey, this might be the right time to take that next step. Although, he will probably expect you to take care of him like his mommy does. If so go to Option #2.

→ OPTION #5

Say goodbye. Dump that mama's boy and get a real man!

87. His parents want to convert you to his religion

You were raised a Catholic, and he was raised Jewish. Neither one of you is religious, and your family doesn't object to you marrying a Jewish guy, and doesn't care if he doesn't convert (you suspect they're just grateful you're getting married at all). But his parents, despite being atheists, feel differently. They need you to convert because, if not, the kids won't be considered Jewish, as Judaism is a matrilineal religion. But you don't want to convert, and you like your Catholic roots. What to do?

→ OPTION #1

Stick to your guns, and your cross. Tell him you love him and you want to marry him but you have no intention of converting. His family wants you to raise the kids Jewish and you wanted a 3-carat engagement ring. You can't always get what you want! And besides, nowadays many families raise their kids with more than one religion. That means Christmas *and* Hanukkah—double the gifts, baby.

→ OPTION #2

Convert, but make a secret deal with God. Tell God that you are only converting because you love your man and you want to marry him, but that in your heart you are still a Catholic. Being all-knowing, he'll know whether you are telling the truth.

→ OPTION #3

Convert him and his family. Good luck with that.

In the Future . . .

Date an atheist.

>>> 88. His parents love your parents ... but your parents hate their guts

It seemed like they all got along fine when they met. They had a lot in common. The same religion. The same socioeconomic background. They grew up in the same place. It seemed that just as you and your boyfriend were a match made in heaven, so too were your parents meant for his parents and vice-versa. But apparently that isn't the case. After their first meeting, your boyfriend's parents keep calling your parents to try to make plans, and sometimes even show up unannounced. His folks seem to think that your folks are their new BFFs. Then your father tells you straight out. "The Andersons? We hate them. God, he is a bore!" Then your mom chimes in. "And that woman. What the hell was she talking about with the whole gardening club thing?"

Uh oh. This can't be good.

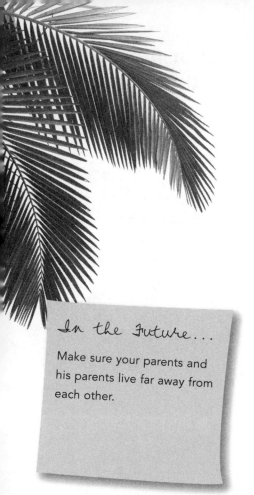

→ OPTION #1

Get his parents to move. Old people should be living in Florida, the top destination for folks on the verge of death, anyway. Get them to buy a condo in the lovely Bella Vista overlooking the sea. It's so nice there, people say you almost forget you're about to die.

→ OPTION #2

Tell your man. I know it is hard, but chances are if his parents are that annoying then maybe he hates them too. Tell him that he has to find a way to persuade his parents to stop pestering yours and that you're sick of being in the middle. Just start yelling and making him feel as though it is his fault. That shit always works on guys.

In the Future . . .

Make sure your parents and his parents live far away from each other.

→ OPTION #3

Make his parents hate yours, too. That way it will be even. There are two ways of doing this. One is to just tell them that your folks don't like them, which unfortunately will inevitably cause them to hate you too. A better way is to start talking shit about your folks to his parents, and make sure your boyfriend does too. That way they will slowly start to feel the same way about your parents that your parents do about them.

→ OPTION #4

Tell your parents to deal. You are no longer a kid, and if they want to be a part of their future grandchild's life they are going to have to hang out with the Andersons and fucking like it.

Hollywood Loves Dysfunctional Families

If you can't get your fam to get along with his, set your sights on the big screen! Just consider:

- *The Royal Tenenbaums*

- *Goodfellas*

- *The Ref*

- *Harold and Maude*

- *Ordinary People*

- *Requiem for a Dream*

- *The Simpsons*

- *Meet the Parents* and *Meet the Fockers*

89. His sister buys you a $4 Christmas gift

Spending the holidays with his family for the first time is a pivotal event in any relationship. It also helps clarify just how much these people love or hate you, depending on what they give you. His parents gave you a beautiful pair of earrings. His brother and his wife gave you an expensive weekend at a revered spa. And you were just as generous. So when you picked up the little cutely wrapped box from his sister you figured you probably scored again. What could it be in such a small package? Another pair of earrings? A ring? A tennis bracelet? You open it up and your eyes pop out of your head. Lip gloss! OMG, is she serious?

→ **STEP #1**

Force a smile. I know you'd rather scowl, but you have to keep your composure. You love your boyfriend after all, and you love the family. Well, most of it! To help you smile when you would rather frown, think of the cheap shitty gift you are going to give her next Christmas—if she lives that long!

→ STEP #2

Say thank you. That's it. I know it is hard to do but get those words out of your mouth with a pair of pliers if you have to. Speaking of pliers, how about that for a gift for her next year?

→ STEP #3

Excuse yourself. Politely, like the lady you are or at least aspire to be. Then go into the bathroom and either cry or scream while plotting your revenge.

→ STEP #4

Let it go. Seriously, throw that cheap ninety-nine-cent lip gloss out. Feel better?

How to Say Thank You Without Saying Thank You

- You: Wow, lip gloss.
- Her: I thought you would like it.
- You: Well, I bet you did. What can I say?
- Her: You're welcome.
- You: I am? Okay then.

OMG in Real Life

My mother-in-law once got me a plate hanger. No plate, just the hanger. The next time I was at her house, I noticed that one of her plates was without a hanger and I realized that bitch took one of her hangers off the wall, wrapped it, and gave it to me. Not the plate, the hanger! My husband didn't want me to say anything, so last year I gave her some of my extra Tupperware lids. Not the containers, just the lids.

—Ann Marie

In the Future . . .

Save all the shitty gifts you get and re-gift them to people you really don't care about. It's okay, you're recycling.

90. His baby mama hates your guts

The baby mama. One of the most difficult things to deal with is when you are dating a guy with kids whose mother is unfortunately still alive. You try to avoid her, but it's impossible. Sometimes you have to pick up the kids when your man is busy, and when you do she always manages to make a snide comment about what you are wearing or the way you did your hair. And the kids, both of whom you love, are constantly being fed terrible things about you. Every time you see them you need to buy them shit to make them like you all over again.

→ **OPTION #1**

Befriend her. Kill her with kindness. Tell the kids how great their mother is over and over again when they come and see you. Inevitably they will tell their mom what you said. Now when she says nasty things about you she'll look like the jerk she is. At least she'll have to be pleasant to you in person.

→ **OPTION #2**

Tell her to take a hike. Hey, he's your man now, not hers. It's not your fault that she turned into a fatty with a bad mouth and a vicious temper. And it's not your fault that she banged that bartender on that Caribbean cruise she went on with your man. She broke his heart; don't let her mess with yours. Fight fire with fire, bitch with bitchier.

→ OPTION #3

Make your man step up and be a man. Why are you dealing with this drama anyway? Tell your man that you are sick and tired of just "ignoring" her because it doesn't work. Tell him that if he loves you he is going to have to grow some balls and march over there and put this woman in her place.

→ OPTION #4

Take your fight to the small screen. Invite this bitch to come on national TV and fight it out while the crowd cheers you on. This way you'll get to speak your mind and whoop her ass at the same time, and hey, you'll be on TV! That's the American dream, isn't it?

In the Future...
Date a guy without kids!

chapter 7

Breaking Up Is Really F#@*ing Hard to Do

91. His Facebook status is "single"—and that's news to you

Oh, no he didn't! Well, actually he did. That's right, the guy you have been dating for the past year, the guy that you love and he said loved you, the guy whose only flaw is that he is almost too good to be true, just dumped your ass—on Facebook! When your friends tell you that your boyfriend just changed his Facebook status from "in a relationship" to "single" you figure it must be some kind of a mistake. Maybe he did it accidentally? Did someone hack his account? So, you message him on Facebook and ask him what the hell is going on. He just says "bye" in the messenger and then blocks you, de-friending you forever. OMG, did he really just break up with you like this?

→ **OPTION #1**

Change your status—quick. You don't want to look like it was you who was dumped. There are some things more important than love—like saving face on a social networking site. Change your status to single and start playing the electronic field.

→ OPTION #2

Send a message to all his friends. Hey, he may have de-friended you but you still have a lot of mutual friends. Post something terrible about him that only you know—something embarrassing like the time he woke up in tears screaming "Mommy!" while sucking his thumb. If there is nothing really embarrassing to tell, just say he has a small penis—even if he doesn't. He'll still be devastated either way.

→ OPTION #3

Lick your wounds. Sure, this one stings. But now you know what kind of guy he really is. Pick yourself up, dust yourself off, and get back out there. Find a super hot new guy and post those pictures all over Facebook, with captions like "Finally, a real guy!" Post it on his friend's page so he sees it.

OMG in Real Life

I was dating this guy for about two weeks when I noticed that he changed his status to "in a relationship." At first I thought, "Wow, this is too soon." Then after a couple of hours, I began to really like the idea. I went back on Facebook to change my status and got a shock. There on his profile were new pictures of him and this other girl kissing and hugging. He was in a relationship, just not with me!

—Tammy

92. You catch him cheating on you

That snake! You had been suspicious of his indiscretions for a while now. For the past few months he hasn't been himself. He never wants to have sex. He never wants to go away for the weekend. He doesn't answer the phone for hours at a time. But what really convinced you he was cheating was his "late nights at the office," particularly since he works from home. Finally, the piece of evidence that even you could not dismiss—him on top of another girl naked on the living room couch as you come home unusually early. OMG!

→ **OPTION #1**

Join in. Don't be such a prude. Maybe that's why he is looking elsewhere for excitement. Ever think of that? Show him (and her) just what you are made of!

→ **OPTION #2**

Scream. At the top of your lungs until all the glasses in the house break and both of them are frozen in fear.

→ **OPTION #3**

Stay calm. Really calm. Like creepy calm. Look at them both and say something like, "Oh, hi, I didn't know we were having company. Let me make a pot of coffee. Who wants some cookies?" This will really freak the shit out of them. Then head into the kitchen and let them imagine the worst.

→ **OPTION #4**

Cry. On your knees, looking up at the sky and cursing the God who betrayed you. Then grab a golf club and start swinging. Hey if it's good enough for Elin. . . .

→ **OPTION #5**

Get out of there. Grab your shit and leave. Don't answer his calls, texts, and so on. Never talk to this pig again. Although make sure you update your status on Facebook to "Getting over a two-timing ass-hole." Make sure his friends see it.

Signs Your Guy Might Be Cheating

- He's extremely vague
- He's acting extra nice for no reason
- He's starting fights for no reason
- Doesn't want sex
- He's always working
- Doesn't answer his phone or return texts
- His friends drop hints
- You catch him screwing another girl

93. You've been broken up for a month and that motherf#@*er already has a girlfriend

"I can't live without you!" "I love you!" "I'll never find love again!" Those were his words as you "stepped on his heart" as he put it, sobbing and screaming that he will never be able to deal with the fact that you and he are no longer an item. Yes, you broke up with him. And yes, he did seem hurt. You felt bad. That is, until you run into him and his new girlfriend at a bar. New girlfriend? Really? It's only been a little over three weeks and he already has a new chick. What happened to the crying and begging and pleading to come back? The late night texts and drunk phone calls asking for one more chance? So much for true love, eh?

→ OPTION #1

Roll your eyes, and laugh. Realize that all guys are far more melo-dramatic than we are even though we are the ones who get that rep. Men. Can't live without them and it really, really sucks to change a tire by yourself.

→ OPTION #2

Get mad. Granted, there really isn't a reason to get upset since you were the one who broke up with him. But since when should you be confined to the prison that is thinking logically? You're a woman, not a robot. He's an ass-hole. Pure and simple.

→ OPTION #3

Get another boyfriend. Two can play at that game. Oh, wait. You already do? Well then WTF are you whining about?

→ OPTION #4

Tell her she's a slut. There is abso-lutely no logical reason for it, but it might make you feel better—and her worse. Which, of course, will make you feel better. Tell her that she is just a rebound and that you are the one he really misses. Then sleep with the next guy who says "hey," to fill the void in your soul.

→ OPTION #5

Calm the F down. See it for what it is, a rebound relationship or an attempt to make you jealous.

94. You woke up hung over . . . and with twenty texts to your ex in your outbox

You slowly open your eyes. Oh, too bright. What time is it? You feel like you swallowed a cat and your head is throbbing. It's official, you're hung over. Your night started at happy hour then just kept going. You decided to celebrate that you're newly single and ready to mingle. You are so over him, and just to prove that to everyone you did ten shots of Jäger. You lie in bed and start to piece the night back together. Then you see it, sitting on your night stand, right next to an empty container of Ben & Jerry's Chunky Monkey—your cell phone. You grab it and start scrolling down to your text messages and there before your eyes is the unthinkable. At *least* twenty text messages to your ex. Starting with, "I am soooo over you," and "I look so hot tonight, too bad for you loser," and ending with "Pleas coem back 2 me, why dnot you love me??!!!" NO!!!!!!!!!!!!

→ OPTION #1

Damage control. Send one last text apologizing for all of the crazy texts the night before. Blame it on an empty stomach and too much booze. Then send it and erase his number from your phone. You've said you're sorry and now you need to move on. And lay off the sauce.

→ OPTION #2

Do nothing. Who cares what he or anyone else thinks? So you sent some drunken texts, join the club. You're only human. Now go out there and find a new guy, that's the best way to get over an ex.

→ OPTION #3

Lie. Call him and blame it on one of your girlfriends. Tell him you had no idea they were sending those texts, because you were too busy hooking up with another guy. Okay, maybe a little immature but so is trying to get over an ex with a bottle of Jägermeister . . . live and learn!

OMG in Real Life

My boyfriend and I had been broken up for almost two months and I thought I was doing great. I went out for a girls' night and I was having a good time, too good I guess. The last thing I remember was sitting in a cab screaming at my best friend "I know he still loves me!" Then the next thing I know, my ex is calling my name. Apparently, I had passed out at his front door. He came home, with another girl, and found me there in his doorway. He called my friends and they came and got me. We never spoke again.

—Elisa

In the Future . . .

Delete your ex's number immediately after you end the relationship. That way even if you're tempted, drunk or sober, you won't be able to contact him.

95. You run into your ex while on a date

Finally you are back on the saddle (i.e., dick) again. Dating, dating, and more dating. Match.com, plentyoffish.com, peoplewithpeniseslookingforpeoplewithvaginas.com. You're on all the sites, and you are making all the right moves. Yep, you are now single and loving it for the first time since your breakup. You're out one night having a great time with the date of the week when you see him across the room. OMG, there is your ex and worse than that—he's on a date. What now?

→ OPTION #1

Make a beeline for the bathroom. Tell your date you have to go to the ladies' room and get the hell out of there before your nerves get the better of you. Splash some water on your face, powder your nose, fix your hair, and, if you really need to, take a couple Valium; then stroll back to the table in your best *America's Top Model* walk. Be graceful and gracious. Basically, be someone else.

→ OPTION #2

Ignore him. Pretend you don't see him and go ahead with your date. Make sure you look like you're having an amazing date, laugh a little louder, flip your hair a little more than usual, and be extra flirty. Make sure he sees you having a much better time on your date than he is on his.

→ OPTION #3

Stick a fork in it. And by it, I mean your ex's eyeball. Just seeing him made you sooo angry!

→ OPTION #4

Introduce your date. To avoid having labels that could piss one of them off like "friend," just say "Bob, this is Todd." Unless, of course, they happen to have other first names.

→ OPTION #5

Ask your ex to join you guys.

In the Future...

Only go on a date to a place where you know your ex can't afford to go. And *always* look amazing just in case.

Just kidding!
What are you, nuts?!

96. Your ex's new girlfriend is your doppelgänger

It took a while but both of you are now at the point where you can be friends since the breakup. The truth is that you both like and respect one another, but you just weren't a good match. So when he reaches out to you a few months after you guys split you are more than willing to be back in his life—as a pal. He even invites you to meet his new girlfriend, which you take to mean that he has finally put the past behind him and he, like you, is over this relationship—ready to finally move on. And then, you see her as you walk into the restaurant. She has your same hair. Same color, same cut. She has the same build, she is the same height. OMG when she smiles you see that she even has the same dimple on her left cheek! Do you have an identical twin you did not know about? This is just too weird. She looks just like you!

→ OPTION #1

Be polite, and keep your mouth shut. Just smile and get through the dinner. Try not to look at her too much, but don't be impolite either. Focus on him—but not too much.

→ OPTION #2

Be flattered. Hey, he obviously still has feelings for you or at least really likes the way you look—especially those dimples! Sure, it's a little creepy but you should take it as a compliment.

→ OPTION #3

Take him back? You were never really sure that he was the one for you but you still have feelings for him—and those feelings just came back and he's obviously still in love with you. When the chick goes to the bathroom, confront him on the fact that his girl is your identical twin. Then ask him if he wouldn't rather have the real thing instead of this cheap imitation. Then apologize for calling her "cheap" and tell him you still love him. Ditch the bitch and leave her to pick up the check—alone.

→ OPTION #4

Call a cop. The man is obviously obsessed with you. Who knows what his next move will be? Run out of there and file a restraining order—stat!

I t had been a while since you last saw your friend, Becky. You used to see each other all the time before you moved a couple hours away after you broke up with your ex. You just had to get away, it made things easier. You've spoken to her a couple times, and the last time you talked she said she was dating someone, but didn't go into much detail.

And then you find out who it is. A mutual friend calls you and gives you the news. "So I guess you heard that Becky is dating your ex?" *What*?!

→ **OPTION #1**

Confront her. Call this Becky bitch up and let her know just how you feel. But first, you have to sit down and figure out just how you do feel. Are you jealous? Do you care? Is it better just to act like you don't care? Maybe she is just doing this because she is jealous of you? Would it piss her off more if you were nonchalant? No, the first one makes more sense. Call this so-called BFF and let her know this is so not cool!

→ OPTION #2

Write an angry letter. That's what my mother always told me to do when I was upset. Then, fold, sharpen, and strengthen the letter into a shank like they do in prison, find her, and stab her. That's what my dad always told me to do when I was upset. FYI—they are no longer married.

→ OPTION #3

Get him back. Show her just who is boss and make him come back to you. Then, you'll find yourself in the same terrible situation that you were in before you moved; shacked up with a guy you don't love.

→ OPTION #4

Jump his best friend. Remember that tall friend of his who always flirted with you? What's his name? Yeah, find him and do him like you've never done anyone before. Make sure your ex finds out about it—it'll drive him nuts.

→ OPTION #5

Start dating one of *her* exes. Shit, start dating all of her exes. Two can play at this game.

→ OPTION #6

Do nothing. If you don't care about this guy anymore then it shouldn't bother you. Maybe they're just more compatible than you guys were. However, she should have told you that she was thinking about dating him before it happened, and you can let her know that. Then let it go and stop living in the past.

In the Future...

Befriend more lesbians—then there's no chance of their ever dating an ex.

98. He's still friends with your friends

Breaking up is hard to do, especially when you can't just disappear on an extended vacation to get some distance and closure. It's easier to get over someone when you are sipping margaritas on a beach in Mexico than taking the train into work every morning, the same train you took with your man every day, a constant reminder of your time together. But it's even worse when you break up with someone who has become friends with all your friends, and you with his. You are bound to run into each other, no matter what you do. OMG, how are you ever going to get over him when he is popping up everywhere you go?

→ OPTION #1

Lay low. Not for good, but for a while. Call and see if he is going to be there when you are meeting friends, and do your best to avoid him. Watch *Dexter* and *Mad Men* with all of your imaginary friends.

→ OPTION #2

Deal with it. Hey, in time, you and he will be able to meet with all your friends, he with his date and you with yours, and you'll have a laugh while you kick around old times. Unfortunately that won't be the case until about 2015.

→ OPTION #3

Get a guy. Doesn't even matter what kind of guy; just make sure you always have a man around when you run into him. You'll feel better, and he'll feel worse. Remember what Gandhi said: "Life is a zero-sum game"—or something like that.

→ OPTION #4

Get new friends. Consider your old ones the casualities of war. Let him have custody of your mutual friends and go out and find new ones. Or just follow Option #3—chances are when you get a new guy, you'll get his friends, too.

→ OPTION #5

Make your friends decide. Let them know that it's either him or you. And if they pick him, then you'll know that you're probably not that great of a friend. Might wanna work on that before making new friends.

In the Future...

When breaking up make sure you decide who gets custody of which friends.

What to Say When You Dump Him

- You deserve more than I can give.
- You're gonna make some girl so happy one day.
- We just don't bring out the best in each other.
- I know one day I will realize that letting you go was the dumbest thing I've ever done.
- I stayed with you this long because you're so amazing.
- It's not forever but for now I need to be alone.

What to Say When He Dumps You

- I agree, we need to break up—because you don't satisfy me sexually.
- Wow, I thought that would hurt, but it doesn't at all.
- Well, all I can say is thank you for being the one to show me what kind of guy I don't want to be with.
- No problem. Truth is I've been seeing someone else, and I was tired of hiding it. Thank you.
- Weird, I was just about to break up with you.
- Okay, no hard feelings. So is it cool if I date your brother then?

>>>> 99. You've been in a relationship for so long, you forgot how to friggin' date

Dating. It sucks but it's either that or dying alone with twenty cats. Yikes! Seriously, that is pretty sad. So while a first date may be torture there is just no other way to meet the man of your dreams. Yep, after a six-year relationship you are thrown back into the dating world. But things have changed so much. Instead of someone calling to ask you out to dinner, a guy writes on your Facebook wall that "Maybe he'll see you at the bar tonight." Has everyone lost their flippin' minds? Or have you turned into an old lady? Either way, you just can't seem to be able to successfully navigate this new, f'd up dating world. What to do?

→ OPTION #1

Grow some balls. Metaphorically—not literally, which is difficult and seriously expensive. Just go out to any local bar or club and strut your stuff on the dance floor. Everyone knows that you meet the best guys in seedy clubs, right?

→ OPTION #2

Grow some boobs. Then follow Option #1 and strut those big fake boobs on the dance floor. The guys will be lining up.

→ OPTION #3

Go online. When you first started dating your ex-boyfriend, only pedophiles and high school kids did online dating. That's true, but times they are a-changing. In fact, they already have. At least on an online dating site you can filter through the losers a little bit. It may not be perfect, but you are probably in a clearer state of mind when you decide to go out with a guy while surfing the net at work than when you're shitfaced and eating a gyro outside a club on a random Saturday night.

→ OPTION #4

Ask your friends. You know, the ones that get all the cute interesting guys? Yeah, might be a good start! They will want to help, especially the ones who have boyfriends, 'cause the last thing they want is for you to come after their men.

→ OPTION #5

Throw a "singles" party. This is a great way for you and maybe your other single friends to meet someone. Tell everyone they have to bring a friend of the opposite sex who is single. Then supply the booze and let it ride (hopefully literally). Worst-case scenario, you'll at least meet a few new friends. Best-case scenario, someone spends the night in your bed!

100. Asshole or not, you just can't get over him

Time usually does heal all wounds. Eventually, a few hundred pounds of chocolate, a dozen boxes of tissues, and a Katherine Heigl movie marathon will usually cure even the worst of broken hearts. If Juliet had gone to a girlfriend's house for wine and chocolate instead of stabbing herself, a few weeks later she'd be alive—and looking for another Romeo. Maybe even one who didn't wear tights.

At least, that's what you thought until you met him. He was the one, and you blew it. It's been months and months and you *still* can't get over him. No matter what you do you can't seem to forget the way he smelled, the way he laughed, or the way his ass looked in jeans.

→ OPTION #1

Lean on your girlfriends, that's what they're for. Let them help you through this shitty time in your life. Also let them help you find your rebound guy.

→ OPTION #2

Stab yourself. Hey, maybe Juliet was right after all. Life without love is not worth living. End it now and forever be at peace. JK. Duh.

→ OPTION #3

Stab him. It's easier to mourn him if he's dead. You'll probably be in prison but they have free counseling in there. JK. Kinda.

→ OPTION #4

Put the dagger down—and get a grip. He's not worth it—hell, no man is. When you really think about it, he wasn't even that tall.

→ OPTION #5

Get hypnosis. Maybe there is a way to forget about him after all? Go to a hypnotherapist and have him erase your memory of this wonderful man of yours. If that doesn't work, according to Dr. House, electroshock therapy can erase all memory of your past. You can still remember to tie your shoes, but you can't remember who the hell you are—let alone who the hell he was. Hey, maybe a fresh start is what you need.

→ OPTION #6

Watch another Katherine Heigl movie.

>>> 101. You still really want to bang him

Sex. Sometimes we ladies like to believe that it is less important to us than it is. But the truth is we will overlook a lot of negative traits in a guy if he knows how to make the kitty purr. Your ex was one of those guys. He may not have been the most ambitious guy . . . or the smartest. Or the nicest. Or the cleanest. But he was good in the sack.

But now it's over and you know you can't be with him. Other than being a master in the bedroom, you don't want to pass on his genes to any future kids. He is, after all, an idiot. But it's been months since you broke up and although you have met some great guys—some of whom were okay between the sheets—you can't help but miss the touch of your ex. Or more specifically, the sex. Damn!

→ OPTION #1

Have some ex sex. Ever heard of friends with benefits? Well, there are also enemies with benefits too. He may hate you, and you may hate him, but we all know there's nothing better than angry sex. Sure, he'll start to cry afterward and curl up into a little ball. That's when you pick him up, carry him outside, and dump him in the street like the dog he is.

→ OPTION #2

Get your ex to make a mold of his tool for you. There are sex shops that specialize in making dildos from a molding of a particular penis. Bring your ex to the shop and get them to make an exact replica of his penis for your enjoyment. Any guy would do this—it would be a tremendous boost to his ego. It may not be as good as the real thing, but at least it won't talk and you won't be forced to have dinner with its parents.

He still calls you.	He changes his number.
He doesn't want you dating anyone.	He has a new girlfriend.
His Facebook status is "In a relationship and it's complicated."	He de-friends you from Facebook.
He shows up drunk at your place.	He gets a restraining order against you when you show up at his place, drunk. Three nights in a row. The last time naked.

→ OPTION #3

Date a relative of his. Like athletic ability, academic excellence, and the ability to fold your tongue in the shape of a taco, sexual proficiency is at least partly hereditary. Chances are his brother or father is just as much of a stud muffin as he is. Unfortunately, being an asshole also runs in the family.

→ OPTION #4

Choose quantity over quality. Yes, the saying usually goes the other way. But, if you can't seem to find a guy who can screw as good as your ex, you might as well go for quantity. Screw everyone, and you're bound to hit on a few good ones here and there.

Art Credits